The world's greatest SEERS & PHILOSOPHERS

Plus the philosophy of *Bhagavad Gita* revealed by Bhagwan Krishna

Clifford Sawhney

Administrative office and sale centre
J-3/16 , Daryaganj, New Delhi-110002
☎ 23276539, 23272783, 23272784 • *Fax:* 011-23260518
E-mail: info@pustakmahal.com • *Website:* www.pustakmahal.com

Branches
Bengaluru: ☎ 080-22234025 • *Telefax:* 080-22240209
E-mail: pustak@airtelmail.in • pustak@sancharnet.in
Mumbai: ☎ 022-22010941, 022-22053387
E-mail: rapidex@bom5.vsnl.net.in
Patna: ☎ 0612-3294193 • *Telefax:* 0612-2302719
E-mail: rapidexptn@rediffmail.com

ISBN 978-81-223-0824-2

Edition: 2013

Printed at : **Radha Offset, Delhi**

Dedication

*To my late beloved Mother,
who worked tirelessly to ensure
her children had the very best
she could afford.*

*To my late beloved Father,
for the countless opportunities created
that sparked a never-say-die spirit
in his greenhorn son.*

ACKNOWLEDGEMENT

Sincere thanks to all the writers who walked the path much before, chronicling the lives of the world's greatest seers and philosophers.

Many thanks to my beloved wife, Monika, for putting up with the hours, days, weeks and months of inattention, when yours truly was glued to the computer console working on this book, instead of spending time with one's better half.

Thanks also to my little daughter, Tanya, for allowing me the liberty of working late into the nights, despite not being able to sleep without papa, and for occasionally staying awake into the wee hours, while desperately trying to keep her sleepy eyes open.

Thanks to Mr Ram Avtar Gupta, MD, Pustak Mahal, for the inspiration to write this book and accepting it for publication. Thanks also to Mr S.K. Roy, Executive Editor, Pustak Mahal, for facilitating the publication of this book and for his whole-hearted support and cooperation. Thanks also to all the other staff members at Pustak Mahal who have made this book possible.

Without all these generous people, this book would never have seen the light of day.

And grateful thanks to the Lord, for all the jokes played upon me, and the trials and tribulations that keep opening one's eyes to the joy of Divine Reality.

CONTENTS

INDIAN PHILOSOPHERS

DIVINE PHILOSOPHY

PREFACE

As the title indicates, this book is all about the world's greatest seers and philosophers. For some readers, the word *seer* may seem somewhat arcane. Simply put, in the context of this book, a 'seer' is one who has had a glimpse of the Ultimate Reality or God. In essence, one who has "seen" the Divine Truth, hence the derivative 'see-er'.

Coming to the word *philosophy*, this is derived from the Greek *philosophia* or "love of wisdom". Philosophy is the rational and critical inquiry and analysis into the basic principles of a discipline. Furthermore, philosophy is divided into four main branches: *metaphysics* – the investigation of the Ultimate Reality; *epistemology* – the study of the origins, validity and limits of knowledge; *ethics* – the study of the nature of morality and prudence; and *aesthetics* – the study of the nature of beauty in the fine arts.

Of course, when the ancient Greeks first spoke about 'philosophy', it referred to the pursuit of knowledge for its own sake. Over millennia, philosophy has embraced all areas of speculative thought, including the arts, sciences and religion. In time, even topics such as mathematics and politics acquired a philosophy of their own.

In this volume, we are primarily concerned with *metaphysics* – the philosophy of spirituality, religion and the Ultimate Reality. That is why, readers will find many celebrated philosophers missing from this list. For those metaphysicians who were towering personalities in their own right and yet haven't made it to these pages, the reasons for the omission could be twofold. Firstly, the data on these persons may have been too sketchy. Secondly, having been blessed with the Divine Vision, their utterances may have been preponderantly 'atheistic', explaining the truth about Cosmic Consciousness in terms that are shocking to the devout, who cannot easily grasp the essence of the Unborn Reality.

For easy reading and comprehension, *The World's Greatest Seers & Philosophers* has been divided into five distinct categories: the Greeks, the Chinese, the Islamic, the Modern and the Indian philosophers.

At the end, there is one name that cannot be categorised, being above all nomenclatures – Sri Krishna. Much before the Greeks had even coined the word *philosophia*, what Sri Krishna revealed was the Ultimate Truth about *Brahman* – the Unborn, Changeless Reality of this cosmos. The Divine Vision that the Lord revealed to the illustrious Arjuna would later be "seen" by seers of subsequent ages, each interpreting the Ultimate Reality or God in his own words. Although every category imparts a flavour all its own, each refers to the same Immortal Truth.

Finally, readers will notice another anomaly – this book of seers and philosophers does not include a single woman. We seek readers' indulgence on this count, too, for much as one would have liked to include at least a couple of female seers, the details of their lives were far too sketchy to do justice for inclusion in this list. Nevertheless, Divine Grace plays no favourites, having been experienced by men and women of all hues. What counts is purely the intensity and passion of the seeker for a communion with God.

We would welcome bouquets and brickbats from readers who wish to express themselves after reading this book. If errors and inconsistencies in text or interpretation come to light, we would be grateful to readers who bring this to our notice. For, much like the Divine, the book of knowledge has no beginning and no end. Therefore, if any inadvertent errors have crept in, we would duly acknowledge the same and rectify this in a future edition.

GREEK PHILOSOPHERS

PYTHAGORAS (580–500 BC)

The Semi-divine Teacher

One of the earliest philosophers to walk this planet, the details of Pythagoras' birth, life and death are shrouded in the mists of time. Pythagoras was born probably around 580 BC in Samos, Ionia, which is on the western coast of present-day Turkey. He was said to have been the son of Mensarchos, a well-to-do man. This Greek religious teacher and philosopher made major contributions in mathematics, astronomy and music.

The early years in Samos were a period of constant strife and warfare. Perhaps because of this state of affairs, he moved to the southern Italian city of Croton about 525 BC. Croton was a relatively safe and peaceful place and it was here that Pythagoras began a religious, philosophical and scientific school. All members of this school were sworn to total secrecy, loyalty and a life of communal living.

Whatever Pythagoreans discovered was always attributed to Pythagoras, even when he was no more! This is the major reason why it has been difficult to decipher what contributions were made directly by Pythagoras and what originated from his followers. Neither did the great man leave any written works. The world – and the philosopher Plato who was greatly influenced by him – are said to have learnt much about Pythagoras' beliefs from a book by the Pythagorean, Philolaus of Tarentum.

Taboos and Divinity

The Pythagorean School was very religious and had many a taboo. For instance, Pythagoreans had to abstain from eating beans, could not pick what had fallen, could never touch a white cock, could not stir fire with iron, could not look into a mirror beside a light, had to remain chaste, wear white clothes and the like. Pythagoras also strictly advocated the cause of vegetarianism, which could be attributed to the fact that he believed in transmigration or rebirth. If one considers the do's and don'ts of the Pythagoreans, it seemed more like a mystical rather than a scientific school.

Indeed, the philosopher considered himself to be a semi-divine mystic and is supposed to have said: "There are men, gods, and men like Pythagoras." Yet, the School was an egalitarian society, where men and women had equal status. All property was supposed to be communal.

Pythagoras' philosophy can be gauged from this statement attributed to him: "There are three kinds of men and three sorts of people that attend the Olympic Games. The lowest class is made up of those who come to buy and sell, the next above them are those who compete. Best of all, however, are those who come simply to look on. The greatest purification of all is, therefore, disinterested science, and it is the man who devotes himself to that, the true philosopher, who has most effectually released himself from the 'wheel of birth'." The philosopher himself believed that he could remember his past lives.

Pythagoras opined that everything in nature, including music and astronomy, could be understood through mathematics and all things had their select number. This belief was to have a crucial bearing on the future development of mathematics and science. Through his mystic experiences, he also gauged that the movement of celestial bodies in the heavens created music, which was referred to as "the Music of the Spheres".

His other important beliefs were that philosophy should be used as a means of spiritual purification and that the soul was destined for heaven and an eventual union with the Divine. The Pythagoreans were always interested in metaphysics or the nature of Being. They believed that the world is composed of opposites (male-female, day-night, wet-dry, hot-cold), a belief also propounded by the Ionians.

Pythagoras preached that there was an eternal world not decipherable by the senses, but revealed only to the intellect. The path to immortality lay in the purification of the soul, which was possible through music and mental activity – a science that would later be termed philosophy. It was through this that one could reach "higher incarnations". With such beliefs, salvation was one of the ideals at Pythagoras' School.

However, as the School gained influence in Croton, it is said to have become politically active, throwing its lot with the aristocracy. This angered the man on the street and turned lay opinion against the Pythagoreans. Matters came to a head when the citizens burned Pythagoras' house, forcing the Pythagoreans to flee to Metapontum, another city in Southern Italy.

The great man spent his last years here, giving up his spirit around 500 BC at the ripe age of 80.

SOCRATES (469–399 BC)

The Father of Western Philosophy

The first of a trio of renowned Greek philosophers (Socrates, Plato, Aristotle) who were responsible for the beginning of modern philosophy, Socrates was born in or around 469 BC. He was the son of Sophroniscus and Phaenarete. His father, Sophroniscus, was said to have been a sculptor.

According to the accounts of Xenophon, Socrates was well versed in geometry and astronomy. Stout in physique, the philosopher was "grotesque" in appearance, with a snub nose, broad nostrils, wide mouth and prominent eyes justifying the unflattering description. However, he was supposedly a good fighting man and "all glorious within". He is said to have had immense self-control and endurance.

Socrates was married late in life to Xanthippe, who bore him three sons. Marriage was apparently not the best of situations for him, for Xenophon speaks of her high temper.

Decrying the fall in moral values during his time, Socrates exhorted people to "know thyself". He rejected the speculative philosophy of the Ionian and Italian philosophers, who indulged in natural and physical speculations. Instead, he repeatedly questioned people about their thoughts and beliefs. He spoke freely with all kinds of people, including poets, artisans, politicians and the layman, investigating their notions and definitions of right and wrong, courage and justice and the like.

Mystical Experiences

A deeply pious man, he nevertheless regarded the mythology of gods as an invention of poets. He held that God's existence is shown not only by the providential order of nature, but also by warning and revelations given in signs, dreams and oracles. Indeed, it was the famous oracle of Apollo at Delphi that is said to have pronounced him the wisest of all men.

Socrates believed in the immortality of the soul. Accounts from Plato indicate he had mystical leanings. According to Plato, he is also said to have heard a "voice" since his childhood, which on occasion forbade him to do certain things. It was these experiences that convinced Socrates that he had a mission from God to make the people aware of their ignorance and the importance of the knowledge of what is good for their soul.

His focus on a spiritual mission meant that he always lived in want. Throughout the year, Socrates is said to have used the same coat and could afford neither shoes nor a shirt. But material wants were not something that unduly bothered a man like Socrates, who had learnt to live within his very limited means. He believed a man should not ruin his life by putting care of the body or "possessions" before the care of one's soul. A man's true self was his soul or psyche, and that is what counted more than anything else. A man's happiness did not depend on material possessions, but on how good or bad his psyche was, the philosopher opined.

Socrates was in military service during the Peloponnesian War. Making mention of Socrates' mystical experiences, Plato talks about one of these, when the philosopher was spellbound in the trenches for 24 hours. Although not a man of politics (he believed it would compromise his principles), in

406–405 BC, however, he became a member of the Boule (legislative council) of 500.

Martyrdom

Yet, the machinations of politicians and his steadfast principles ultimately proved to be his undoing. At the trial of the victors of Arginusae, he was pressurised to join the unconstitutional condemnation of the generals. He resisted. In 404 BC, the oligarchy of the Thirty Tyrants in Athens asked him to arrest Leon, one of their victims, in order to implicate him in their proceedings. Once again, Socrates refused to oblige.

His refusal to compromise on his principles meant Socrates was making powerful enemies. In 399 BC, Socrates was indicted for "impiety", "corruption of the young" and "neglect of the gods whom the city worships and the practice of religious novelties". The prosecutors pressed the death charges.

Socrates could have made a proper defence. However, he chose to treat the charges with contempt, which incensed his prosecutors, who voted for the death penalty by a majority. The philosopher, though, seemed unperturbed by this turn of events. He was condemned to death by the drinking of hemlock, a deadly plant poison.

Since there was a delay of a month in his execution, while the arrival of the poison was awaited, his friends urged him to escape. Socrates would have none of this, though, contending that although the verdict was not justified, it was passed by a legitimate court and must therefore be carried out.

When his last hours drew near, he was as calm and composed as ever and drank the potion without hesitation. Thus ended the life of Greece's greatest philosopher. Along with the *Dialogues* of Plato, which had Socrates as the central character, it was martyrdom that helped raise his stature to the level of an icon.

❑ ❑ ❑

PLATO (428–347 BC)

The World of Ideas

The youngest son of Ariston and Perictione, Plato was born in 428 BC in Athens (some accounts put his birthplace as Acgina), Greece. His childhood name was said to have been Aristocles. It was during his school days that he was dubbed *Platon* ("broad") because of his broad shoulders.

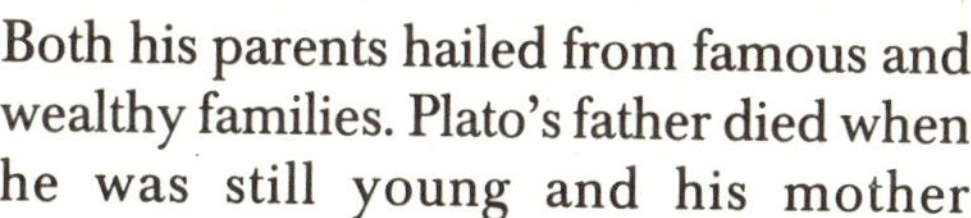

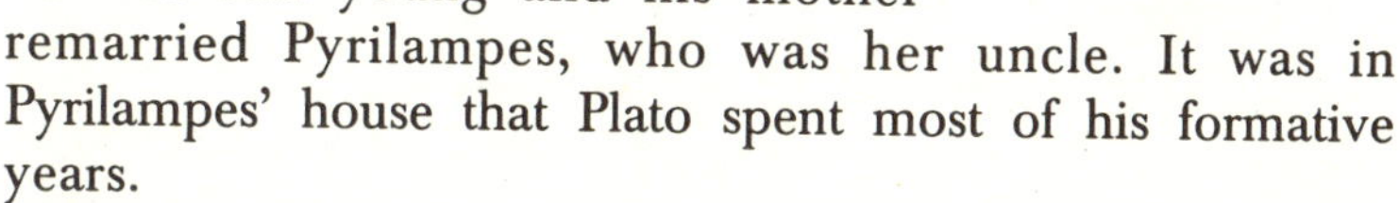

Both his parents hailed from famous and wealthy families. Plato's father died when he was still young and his mother remarried Pyrilampes, who was her uncle. It was in Pyrilampes' house that Plato spent most of his formative years.

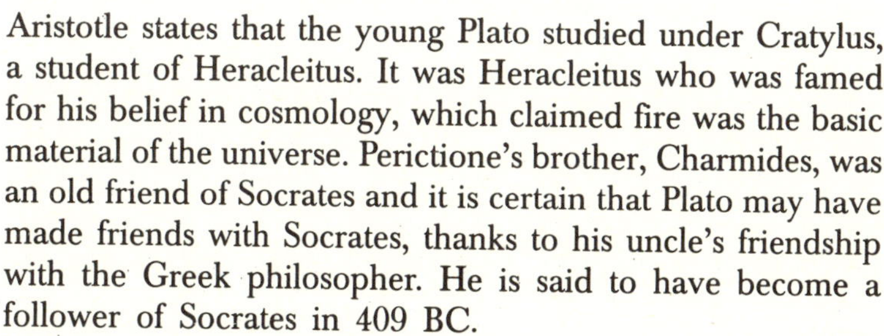

Aristotle states that the young Plato studied under Cratylus, a student of Heracleitus. It was Heracleitus who was famed for his belief in cosmology, which claimed fire was the basic material of the universe. Perictione's brother, Charmides, was an old friend of Socrates and it is certain that Plato may have made friends with Socrates, thanks to his uncle's friendship with the Greek philosopher. He is said to have become a follower of Socrates in 409 BC.

Although Plato's early ambitions were purely political, he was forced to enter military service when the Peloponnesian War was fought between Athens and Sparta (431–404 BC). Plato underwent military service from 409 to 404 BC. When the war ended, he joined the oligarchy of the Thirty Tyrants in Athens set up in 404 BC. He was just 24 and keen on entering public life.

However, although one of its leaders happened to be Charmides, Plato left the oligarchy in a hurry when it fell into violent acts.

This was all the better for Plato, because the Tyrants soon implicated Socrates in the illegal killing of a victim. In 403 BC, democracy was restored in Athens and Plato was once again hopeful of realising his political ambitions. However, Socrates was soon condemned to death by the Tyrants.

When Socrates was executed in 399 BC, Plato's faith was shaken to the core. He now concluded that there was no place in active politics for any man of conscience and decided to stay away from politics, opining that until "kings were philosophers or philosophers were kings" things would never go well with the world.

Plato and other disciples of Socrates then took refuge at Megara with Euclid, who was the founder of the Megarian School of philosophy. Over the next few years, he travelled extensively through Greece, Egypt, Sicily and Italy. It was in Egypt that he first heard of the water clock and later introduced it into Greece.

Talking about his visit to Sicily and Italy at the age of 40, Plato revealed that he was disgusted by the gross sensuality of life in these places. However, he said he found a kindred spirit in Dion, brother-in-law of Dionysius I, the tyrant of Syracuse.

In Italy, he also learnt of the work of Pythagoras. It was here that he came to appreciate the value of mathematics. This was to have deep implications for, in his words, "...the reality which scientific thought is seeking, must be expressible in mathematical terms, mathematics being the most precise and definite of thinking which we are capable of". This idea was to have an immense influence on the development of science from its very beginning to the present day.

The Academy

Plato later returned to Athens and in about 387 BC or soon thereafter, he opened a school of learning on land that belonged to a man called Academus; hence, the school was called the Academy. This is a term that is still used to denote a school or university. It is said that Plato set up the Academy in order to train young men in the art of becoming just and fair statesmen – a move that may have been prompted by his bitter experience with Athenian politics.

Plato's Academy was devoted to systematic research and instruction in philosophy and the sciences. Over the years, with Plato presiding over it, the Academy became a recognised authority in mathematics and jurisprudence also. The importance Plato accorded mathematics comes through from his belief that it provides the finest training for the mind. Which is why, the door of the Academy bore the legend:

Let no one unversed in geometry enter here.

In 367 BC, after the death of Dionysius I, Plato went to Syracuse on the invitation of Dion, who asked him to tutor the new ruler, Dionysius II. Dion believed that if his brother-in-law were trained in science and philosophy, he would be able to prevent Carthage from invading Sicily. Although Plato was sceptical of the plan, he still went to Syracuse. The plan, however, fell apart when Dionysius II drove Dion out of Syracuse, as he was jealous and fearful of Dion's influence.

Thereafter, Plato returned to Athens. Between 361 and 360 BC, Plato visited Syracuse for the second time, trying his best to bring the rivals together, at some personal risk, without success. Dion then attacked and captured Syracuse in 357 BC. But in 354 BC, Dion was murdered.

After Dion's murder, Plato wrote *Epistles vii* and *viii*, in which he reviewed and justified the policies followed by Dion and himself and made proposals (they were unsuccessful) for a reconciliation between the warring parties in Sicily. He also wrote many other works during this period.

Works and Beliefs

Plato's main works focused on philosophy, mathematics and science. Plato wrote around 30 "dialogues", which were a series of discussions between Socrates and others. It is believed that Plato may have begun writing his dialogues around the time he began his Academy.

Since Plato never actually introduced himself in any of these dialogues, it is difficult to conjecture which views are those of Socrates and which of Plato.

It was through his dialogues that Plato wrote a lot on the theory of art, particularly music, dance, drama, poetry and architecture. In philosophy, he discussed a range of topics that included ethics and metaphysics, where he talked of man, mind, realism and immortality. He also discussed logic and legal philosophy, including rhetoric. In religious philosophy, the discussions revolved around atheism, dualism and pantheism. Plato's ideas were later to become permanent elements in Western philosophy.

His philosophy rests on his famous Theory of Ideas (also called the Doctrine of Forms), in which Plato rejected the changeable, deceptive world that we perceive through our senses and propounded his "world of ideas", which he held were constant and true. This theory also speaks of the "tripartite soul" and that knowledge is a "recollection".

The Two Realms

The Theory of Ideas is expressed repeatedly in his dialogues in the *Republic* and the *Parmenides.* Plato opined that existence was in two realms, an "intelligible realm" and a "sensible realm". The intelligible realm comprises perfect, eternal and invisible Ideas or Forms. The sensible realm consists of concrete, familiar objects such as trees, animals, human bodies and other material objects that can be perceived through the senses, but which are actually unreal, shadowy and imperfect copies of the Ideas.

This concept was based on the fact that all objects perceived by the senses undergo constant change. Therefore, any assertion made about these objects at one point of time will not hold good later. These objects, Plato held, are not totally real, but only appeared so to the senses. Therefore, beliefs based on the experience of such objects are unreliable.

Against this, the principles of mathematics and philosophy were real knowledge, as these were discovered through inner meditation on the Ideas.

Plato put the point across forcefully in the *Republic*, where he described humanity as being imprisoned in a cave and mistaking shadows on the wall for reality. It was only philosophers who penetrated the world of reality lying outside the cave of ignorance, thereby achieving insight into true reality, the realm of Ideas.

In his main work dealing with scientific questions, the *Timaeus*, Plato states clearly that this universe "in very truth [is] a living creature with soul and reason".

The *Republic*, the greatest of all Plato's dialogues, combines ethical, political, aesthetic, mystical and metaphysical issues. The *Phaedo* is devoted to metaphysical themes, the *Protagoras* to ethical and political issues and the *Symposium* to aesthetic and mystical themes. In the *Phaedo*, Plato's faith in "personal immortality" shines through. This is a reference to the divinity of the soul, which survives death.

In 347 BC, at the age of 80, Plato is said to have passed away while attending the marriage feast of one of his students. He was subsequently buried in the Academy.

The Academy was an active institution until 529 AD, when Roman Emperor Justinian ordered its closure, terming it a "pagan" establishment. The Academy had survived for an incredible 900 years, the longest any university has ever survived!

ARISTOTLE (384–322 BC)

The Peripatetic Teacher

One of the greatest philosophers of all time who contributed to the rise of modern philosophy, Aristotle was born in the summer of 384 BC at Stagirus, a small Greek colony in the Thracian peninsula of Chalcidice, northern Greece. His father was Nicomachus, a court physician to Amyntas III, the King of Macedonia, who was the grandfather of Alexander the Great. Aristotle's mother was Phaestis, who belonged to a family from Chalcis in Euboea.

The position of court physician being hereditary, Aristotle was introduced to the Greek medical traditions of Hippocrates, the father of modern medicine, from an early age. This knowledge was to come in handy in the biological research he carried on later in life. As per the traditions of those times, it was understood that Aristotle too would take to medicine.

In those days, people never visited doctors. Rather, the doctors were itinerant, travelling from one place to the other, tending the sick. There is little doubt that Aristotle may have been his father's travelling companion.

Turbulent Years

However, details of Aristotle's early life are rather hazy and give no indication whether he lived with his father in Pella, Macedonia's capital city, where his father served King Amyntas. It is possible that Aristotle came in contact with Philip II, the father of Alexander the Great, here.

When he was barely ten, Aristotle's father expired. With his mother also having passed away when he was very young, the young boy thereafter lived with Proxenus of Atarneus, who was probably a relative of his father. It was Proxenus who then taught the boy Greek, rhetoric and poetry.

In 369 BC, the King of Macedonia, Amyntas, died and the kingdom was beset with internal and external strife. At the age of 17 in 367 BC, Aristotle was enrolled at Plato's Academy in Athens. He spent the next 20 years here, attending Plato's lectures. In subsequent years, Aristotle began teaching at the Academy, with rhetoric said to be one of the subjects.

With Plato's death some time around 347 BC, the master's nephew Speusippus was appointed to head the Academy. Soon, Aristotle left the Academy and began travelling. Some accounts say he left because he was peeved at not being made the head of the Academy, but this may not be true. What seems more likely is that he was forced to leave after Philip sacked the Greek city-state of Olynthus in 348 BC and annexed Chalcidice, leading to intense anti-Macedonian feelings. Aristotle's birthplace, Stagirus, held out for a while, before succumbing to the forces of Philip. Thanks to Aristotle's friendship with Philip and his Macedonian links, the Greeks now probably regarded him with suspicion.

For the next 12 years, Aristotle kept travelling with a close circle of friends, which included Xenocrates of Chalcedon and Theophrastus of Eresus. Aristotle first went to Assus, a newly built town on the Asian side of the Aegean. Here the ruler, Hermeias of Atarneus, a Greek mercenary who had managed to acquire control of the area, received him. Having visited the Academy in Athens, Hermeias had invited two of

Plato's graduates to set up a new intellectual centre that would help spread Greek philosophy on the Asian side. Naturally, Aristotle settled here for some time.

It was here that he happened to be attracted to Pythias, who was either the niece or adopted daughter of Hermeias. They were soon married and she bore him one child, a daughter who was also named Pythias. When they married, Pythias may have probably been around 18 years of age and much younger to Aristotle, who was 37. His marital years were probably some of the best, for in his Will he wrote: "Wherever they bury me, there the bones of Pythias shall be laid, in accordance with her own instructions."

This was not to be, though. A decade after their marriage, Pythias died. Not long thereafter, Aristotle chose Herpyllis (who belonged to his hometown, Stagirus) as his companion. Although they were never united in holy matrimony, she bore him a son, Nicomachus. Without doubt, these years of companionship were happy ones for Aristotle.

Independent Stance

It was probably in Assus that he began work on two of his treatises, *Politics* and *On Kingship*. His philosophical leanings now began to take an independent stance from Plato's. Along with his research into plant and animal life, he also began reflecting on the relation of the soul with the body. Here again, he differed with his mentor, Plato, who had opined that the soul was an entity independent of the body, simply using the body as a temporary residence. Aristotle stated that the soul was the vital principal essentially united with the body to form an individual person. He also believed that the heavenly bodies were composed of ether, an imperishable substance, and were moved by God perpetually in perfect circular motion.

But his years of peace at Assus came to an end when the Persians attacked the town. Hermeias was captured and killed, forcing Aristotle to flee to the nearby island of Lesbos. He remained there for a year. Settling in the capital city of Mytilene, with his friend Theophrastus he is said to have established a philosophical circle. It was now that he began his biological research, undertaking pioneering investigations. His strong interest in the structure and anatomy of living beings was thanks to the early years of medical learning with his father. His studies are said to have laid the foundations of the biological sciences and held good for more than two millennia.

Thereafter, he proceeded to Macedonia, which was now at peace with Athens, after a treaty signed with Philip in 346 BC. Aristotle made his way to the Court of Macedonia in 343 or early 342 BC, where some accounts state that he was then appointed the tutor of Philip's 13-year-old son, Alexander. When Alexander later came to power, he would protect Aristotle's Academy.

After three years at the Macedonian Court, Aristotle then went to his hometown Stagirus in 339 BC. In 335 BC, when he was nearly 50 years old, he returned to Athens. Around this time, the death of Speusippus meant that the opportunity to head the Academy was once again open. Yet again, he was passed up and Xenocrates was elected the head.

The Lyceum

This time around, he definitely felt slighted. Soon thereafter, he founded his own school of philosophy, the Lyceum. He is said to have lectured on numerous topics - physics, astronomy, meteorology, zoology, logic, metaphysics, theology, psychology, politics, economics, ethics, rhetoric and poetry. What is astounding is that most of these subjects did not exist before his time! It was largely due to his lectures, which defined the basic principles, that these subjects came to be established as systematic disciplines.

For the next 12 years, he would give instructions while walking up and down the *peripatos*, a covered walkway. It was not long before that the school was referred to as the Peripatetic School, thanks to the philosopher's habit of walking to and fro while teaching his students. During these years, he gave numerous lectures on scientific and philosophical issues. In a series of works under the title *Organon*, Aristotle set forth the laws by which human understanding was said to effect conclusions from the particular to the knowledge of the universal.

However, his Peripatetic School considered philosophy the exclusive preserve of the learned class. They held that such knowledge lay only within the grasping capacity of the Greeks, with their supposed racial superiority entitling them to lord over the non-Greek tribal people, who were treated as serfs or slaves. This insular thinking withheld the benefits of his philosophy from a much wider audience.

False Charges

On the death of Alexander the Great in 323 BC, anti-Macedonian feelings once again swept Athens, briefly but strongly. Yet again, Aristotle fell a victim to the perception that he was a Macedonian sympathiser. This was despite the fact that relations between Alexander and Aristotle had later turned frosty after the former executed the philosopher's nephew, historian Callisthenes of Olynthus, in early 328, while he was accompanying the conqueror in Persia to chronicle his campaign.

Just as Socrates had been indicted decades ago, Aristotle was charged with "impiety", on the specious grounds that a poem he had penned on the execution of King Hermeias by the Persians happened to be an arrant deification. The actual reason, however, was political and linked to his contacts with the Macedonian leader, Antipater.

Unlike Socrates, Aristotle was not willing to play the martyr. Along with his disciples, Aristotle fled to Chalcis in Euboea, north of Athens, commenting that he abandoned Athens as he didn't want its citizens to sin twice against philosophy, an allusion to the execution of Socrates on similar grounds.

A year later, in 322 BC, he passed away at the age of 62, reportedly from a stomach ailment. From amongst his large number of works, only around 22 now survive.

CHINESE PHILOSOPHERS

LAO TZU (570–490 BC)

The Way of Nothing

The ancient Chinese philosopher Lao Tzu's life story is shrouded in mystery. Considered the first philosopher of the Taoist school (*Tao-chia*), his precise date of birth is not known. Scholars place his birth anywhere between 300 and 600 BC, with some accounts putting it around 570 BC, in the province of Henan. Believed to be a court librarian, he is credited with the writing of the philosophical treatise, *Tao-te Ching* (*Classic of the Way and Its Virtue*). *Tao* means *the way of all life*, *te* implies *virtue* or *the proper use of life by men*, and *ching* denotes *text* or *classic.*

In fact, Lao Tzu wasn't even his real name, but an honorific meaning 'Old Master'. His name at birth was said to be Li Erh. While sages like Shen Tao (who asked people to 'abandon knowledge and discard self') first began speaking of the Tao, it was with Lao Tzu that Taoism as a philosophy and way of life really began to take root.

Some scholars contend that Lao Tzu was actually an older contemporary of Confucius. Yet others contend that *Tao-te Ching* is a compilation of paradoxical poems that were really written by several Taoists under the pseudonym, Lao Tzu. It is the most translated Chinese work and teaches that "the way" is realised by recognising and accepting "nothingness".

Taoism believes the universe operates as per the Tao, which is beyond all verbal and intellectual comprehension. As the Master put it, experience of the Tao can be realised through *kuan* (silent contemplation of nature) and *wu-wei* (the absence of mental and physical strain).

Essentially, wisdom lies in understanding that weakness is truly akin to strength, that happiness depends on disaster and passivity is the greatest action.

While the sage's wise words ensured there was no dearth of followers, he refrained from putting his ideas down in writing, fearing that it would not be long before written words turned into formal dogmas. This was not something Lao Tzu would have welcomed, as he believed his doctrines should remain a natural way of life that was lived with good intentions.

Laying down no rigid behavioural codes, he said that a person's conduct should be governed by his instinct and conscience.

Go with the Flow

He held that like every other thing in the universe that was constantly influenced by external forces, so too was human life. All straining or striving was not only meaningless, but counterproductive too. Instead, he averred, one should be spontaneous and endeavour to do nothing (*wu-wei*). This was possible by forsaking knowledge, which meant abandoning names, distinctions, tastes and desires.

It is important, however, to understand what Lao Tzu's concept of *wu-wei* was, in order to grasp the essence of his teaching. By this the philosopher did not mean literally doing nothing. What he meant was one had to discern, understand and then follow the natural forces. In other words, one should follow the tide and thereby try to regulate the flow of events, rather than attempt to flow against the natural order of things, which was bound to be futile. For this, one had to be spontaneous in action.

It is this mindset that is prevalent in the Chinese system of *Tai-chi Chuan*, where the body movements and exercises are soft, smooth and flowing, leaving one feeling refreshed and energised, unlike other exercise systems that leave the practitioner feeling drained!

Essentially, Taoist philosophy sought to accomplish everything by doing nothing. Taoism rejected the Confucian thought of attempting to regulate one's life and society, instead advising adherents to move to a solitary contemplation of nature. By doing this, one could finally gain Ultimate Knowledge and thereby harness the infinite powers of the universe.

In the words of Lao Tzu:

> *The Tao abides in non-action*
>
> *Yet nothing is left undone.*
>
> *If kings and lords observed this,*
>
> *The ten thousand things would develop naturally.*
>
> *If they still desired to act,*
>
> *They would return to the simplicity of formless substance.*
>
> *Without form there is no desire.*
>
> *Without desire there is tranquillity.*
>
> *In this way all things would be at peace.*

Strangely, with thoughts like these, Taoist philosophy was able to reach out to rulers and advise them on how to govern their domains successfully. Although not meant to be a political philosophy per se, in some ways, it did become one. The reason for this can be understood from the following lines:

The Taoist sage has no ambitions, therefore he can never fail. He who never fails, always succeeds. And he who always succeeds is all-powerful.

Lao Tzu urged his followers to lead their lives with simplicity, observation, intuition and love, never resorting to force. Unlike Confucianism, which was more concerned with social relations, human conduct and society, Taoism had a more individualistic, mystical streak that was heavily influenced by nature.

Human pursuits were futile, the philosopher stressed:

The five colours blind the eye.
The five tones deafen the ear.
The five flavours dull the taste.
Racing and hunting madden the mind.
Precious things lead one astray.

The Unfathomable

This was why one should be guided by what one feels and not by what he sees. In a way, the term *Tao* had mystical connotations that referred to the unfathomable source of all life, as comes through in these lines:

Look, it cannot be seen – it is beyond form.
Listen, it cannot be heard – it is beyond sound.
Grasp, it cannot be held – it is intangible.
These three are indefinable; they are one.

In all these lines, there is no doubt the philosopher is referring to what the Vedic seers termed *Brahman.* The following lines are another pointer in this direction:

From above it is not bright;
From below it is not dark;
Unbroken thread beyond description.
It returns to nothingness.
Form of the formless,
Image of the imageless,
It is called indefinable and beyond imagination.
Stand before it – there is no beginning.
Follow it and there is no end.
Stay with the Tao,
Move with the present.

Like many facts about him, Lao Tzu's end is also shrouded in mystery. Legend has it that at the end of his long life, he was saddened by the evil ways of men and their unwillingness to follow the path of natural goodness. Deciding to leave it all behind, he sat astride his water buffalo and rode towards the gate of the Great Wall protecting the Chou dynasty on the western borders of China. At the Hsien-ku Pass, Yin Hsi (the legendary guardian of the pass) begged him to record the teachings of his philosophy for posterity.

This is when Lao Tzu wrote a book of 5,000 characters, divided into two sections, setting down his thoughts on the Tao. This was the legendary book of 81 sayings, the *Tao-te Ching.* After the Bible, this ancient Chinese text is the world's most translated book. Having fulfilled the gatekeeper's request, Lao Tzu then left and "nobody knows what has become of him", according to the account of Ssu-ma Ch'ien, an ancient Chinese historian. Which seems befitting for China's most enigmatic seer.

❑ ❑ ❑

CONFUCIUS (551–479 BC)

China's Supreme Sage

The Chinese philosopher and teacher, Ch'iu K'ung, later to become famous as K'ung-fu'-tse (Confucius), or K'ung the Philosopher, was born in the state of Lu (present-day Shandong Province) in China in 551 BC. Belonging to the noble K'ung clan, his father was a commander of a district in Lu.

Confucius' father died when he was barely three years old and the family was left utterly destitute. But naturally, he was brought up in difficult circumstances under the loving care of his widowed mother and grew up a self-educated man. As a young boy, he was said to be fond of setting up sacrificial vessels and imitating the gestures of rituals.

Around the age of 15, he was consumed by the urge for learning – an urge that was to remain with him throughout his life. By the age of 19, he was married.

In the next few years, a son and two daughters were born to him. However, his relations with his wife and children were not very cordial. A large, strong man around the time of his marriage, he was then serving as a superintendent of parks and herds in a noble family.

Studies and Travel

His mother died in 527 BC. After observing a period of mourning, he took to teaching as a career. He usually travelled around, teaching the small number of disciples who were beginning to flock to him. Soon, word spread about this man of learning and character, especially his reverence for Chinese ideals and customs.

When he was 32, he began teaching ancient rituals to a minister's sons. A year later, he went to the imperial capital, Lo-yang, to study the customs and traditions of the Chou Empire (1027–256 BC). By now the Chou Empire was said to have split into many warring states and the capital city was merely a religious centre. Around this time, he was supposed to have visited the sage Lao Tzu.

When Confucius was 34, powerful rivals among the local nobility threatened the Prince of Lu, who was forced to flee the city. Confucius also accompanied the prince to a neighbouring state. It was here that Confucius learned to play music and become so absorbed in it that he would forget to eat!

On his return to Lu some time later, he devoted the next 15 years to his studies. This was the time when feudalism had degenerated in China. Vice and intrigue were a part of life. Deploring the disorder and abysmal moral standards, Confucius felt the only solution lay in converting people to the principles preached by the sages of yore. Towards this end, he taught his pupils the ancient classics and stressed the immense value of personal example. Rulers could only be great if they themselves led exemplary moral lives. Only then could their kingdom become prosperous and happy, he stressed.

At 51, he returned to political life and had an opportunity to implement his theories. He was first appointed Magistrate of Chung-tu. The next year, he became Minister of Justice of the state of Lu. He introduced reforms, ensured justice was dispensed quickly and fairly and saw to it that crime was almost eliminated.

By this time, the Prince of Lu was becoming increasingly powerful, overcoming the nobles who had previously opposed him. Alarmed by this, a neighbouring prince sent the Prince of Lu a gift of 80 beautiful girls trained in dancing and music and a troop of the best horses. In return, he is said to have sought the dismissal of Confucius.

Enamoured by the girls, the prince thereafter neglected his kingdom and the counsel of Confucius.

Fruitless Search

After having given four of his best political years at Lu, Confucius resigned from his position and left the city in 496 BC. For the next 12 years between the ages of 56 to 68, he wandered from state to state travelling and teaching, hopeful that he would be called back or be able to practise his political doctrines elsewhere.

Confucius had firm views on the art of governance and believed that the personal character and conduct of the ruler was very important. Responding to a prince on a related query, Confucius said: "To govern is to set things right. If you begin by setting yourself right, who will dare to deviate from the right?"

In 484 BC at the age of 68, he finally returned home to Lu, lamenting that after wandering in nine provinces, there was still no goal in sight for him and his search for an ideal ruler had proved fruitless. His last few years in Lu were spent relatively quietly. He is said to have studied the *I Ching*, laid the groundwork for a new educational system and committed traditions to writing by instructing a group of young disciples.

Although Confucius may not have had the influence befitting his stature during his lifetime, in the years to come, his teachings would live on and Confucianism would become a way of life, a philosophy and a religion, in China.

Confucius always preached that man should achieve sagehood through self-cultivation and inner enlightenment. He advocated the development of *jen*, which has been interpreted as love, magnanimity and compassion. When his disciples asked him what he meant by *jen*, he simply said: "Love men." The other qualities he stressed were *te* (virtue) and *yi* (righteousness). This is what differentiated a "superior man" from an inferior man. The Chinese sage said: "The superior man is concerned with virtue; inferior man is concerned with land."

Throughout his life, Confucius walked the talk, and at the end of his long innings, he confessed: "At 15, I set my heart on learning; at 30, I was firmly established; at 40, I had no more doubts; at 50, I knew the will of Heaven; at 60, I was ready to listen to it; at 70, I could follow my heart's desire without transgressing what was right."

Although he prayed, fasted and attended sacrifices, he vigorously opposed popular religious practices, for instance, the animistic cult that derived from the Yin dynasty, which had degenerated into witchcraft and sorcery.

He stressed obedience to the "Mandate of Heaven". In his discourses, the sage always avoided religion, teaching his disciples all about ethics.

Ethical, Not Religious

The crux of the Master's teachings centres on the *tao* or the Mandate of Heaven. Confucius believed that there is an absolute principle underlying the universe, which is moral and ethical, not mystical. Confucius' interpretation of *tao* was as a way of action, of living. An individual was supposed to cultivate himself to achieve *tao* and this talent and virtue were, in turn, made available for his fellow human beings so that the Mandate of Heaven would prevail in the world.

Rather than being religious, his teachings were more practical and ethical. He said human duty should be based on the five virtues of kindness, uprightness, decorum, wisdom and faithfulness. He stressed that in society, a man should be conscious of his obligations, rather than his rights and prerogatives. Confucians exhort the individual through the words, "Sageness within and kingliness without." In short, a man should adopt the Middle Path by being both, a man of spiritual enlightenment and a man of worldly affairs.

Confucius is said to have had a premonition of his death one morning, saying: "The great mountain must collapse, the mighty beam must break and the wise man wither like a plant."

Eight days later, at the age of 73, Confucius was no more.

Lasting Influence

He is supposed to have compiled and edited the *Ch'un Ch'iu* (*Spring and Autumn Annals*), an annalistic account of Chinese history in the state of Lu from 722 to 481 BC. Along with those of his main disciples, his teachings are outlined in the *Shih Shu* (*Four Books*) of Confucian literature, which became the textbooks of subsequent Chinese generations.

A century after Confucius' death, the rise of Mencius (371–289 BC), regarded as the Second Sage, led to a vigorous revival of Confucius' teachings. It was Mencius who gathered all the sayings and discourses of Confucius into books, the most popular of which is *Lun Yu* (*Conversations*), also known as *The Book of Analects*. Consisting of 20 sections and 496 chapters, it is a collection of the discourses, conversations and travels of the Master that had been kept by his disciples. Chinese regard this as the Scripture of Confucianism and the most reliable source of the Master's teachings. These teachings soon led to Confucius being hailed as China's Supreme Sage.

In the centuries to come, the influence of Confucianism would spread to Korea, Japan and Annam (present-day Vietnam).

ISLAMIC PHILOSOPHERS

AL-FARABI (870–950 AD)

The Second Master

The Islamic philosopher Muhammad ibn Tarkhan ibn Uzalagh al-Farabi (also known as Abu al-Nasr al-Farabi) was born of Turkish parents in the small village of Wasij near Farab, Turkistan (now in Uzbekistan) in 870 AD. His parents were of Persian descent, but their ancestors had migrated to Turkistan. Farabi's father was a general.

His early schooling was at Farab and Khorasan (present-day Iran). Later, he went to Baghdad for higher studies, where his Syrian Christian teachers taught him Greek philosophy. Between 901 and 942 AD, Farabi studied and worked in Baghdad. Those were the years when he acquired proficiency in several languages and over different branches of knowledge.

Thanks to the Greek influence, al-Farabi was one of the first Muslim thinkers to convey the teachings of Plato and Aristotle to the Islamic world. This was to exert a tremendous influence on later Islamic philosophers such as Ibn Sina (Avicenna) and Ibn Rushd (Averroes). Farabi believed that a Supreme Being had created the universe through the exercise of rational intelligence. He held that it was this very rational intelligence that was also present in humans and the only aspect of humans that happened to be immortal. He opined that the primary goal for humans, therefore, was to ensure the development of this rational faculty.

In the pursuit of learning and knowledge, he travelled to distant lands, living in Egypt and Damascus for some time, before returning to Baghdad. Farabi ultimately settled down at the court of the ruler of Aleppo (present-day Syria) Saif al-Daulah (916–67 AD). He became one of the constant companions of the king and soon made a name for himself. In the initial years, he held the post of a *qazi* (judge). Later on, he turned to teaching for his living. Suffering great hardships later in life, he even became the caretaker of a garden, at one point.

He was the first Islamic philosopher to state that philosophical truths were the same throughout the world and he held them to be above revelations and religious laws. He believed that the different religions of the world were symbolic expressions of an ideal universal religion.

Literary Contributions

A prolific writer, although many of his works have been lost due to the ravages of history and time, at least 117 of his works have been identified. Of these, 43 are on logic, 11 on metaphysics, seven each on ethics and political science, 17 on music, medicine and sociology, while 11 happen to be commentaries. His commentaries on Aristotle led to him earning the sobriquet "the Second Master" (the first being Aristotle).

One of his most famous books is the *Fusus al-Hikam*, which was a textbook on philosophy for centuries at various Islamic institutions and is taught even today at some centres of the Islamic world. His book *Ara Ahl al-Madina al-Fadila* (*The Model City*) was a major early contribution to sociology and political science.

Another book, *Catalogue of Sciences*, is a unique treatise on the classification and fundamental principles of science. He attempted to systematise human knowledge through this compilation, the first such work of its kind by a Muslim thinker. Besides these works, al-Farabi's *Great Book of Music* is another important literary contribution of that era. Many of his works are today preserved in medieval Latin translations only.

Through his treatises, he made an immense contribution to philosophy, science, logic, sociology, medicine, music and mathematics. Farabi made the study of logic easier by dividing it into two categories, *Takhayyul* (idea) and *Thubut* (proof).

A bachelor all his life, al-Farabi passed away at Damascus in 950 AD, at the ripe old age of 80.

❑ ❑ ❑

IBN SINA (980–1037 AD)

The Doctor of Doctors

Abu Ali al-Husain ibn Abdullah ibn Sina – famous in the West as Avicenna – was born in Afshaneh near Bukhara (Uzbekistan). His father, Abdullah, was from Balkh and his mother was a native of a village near Bukhara. His early education was through his father, an Ismaili, an Islamic religious and political movement. By the age of ten he is said to have mastered much of the *Koran* and various sciences, thanks to his photographic memory. Yet, his thoughts were too eclectic for him to be attracted to the Ismaili outlook.

Thereafter, he began studying philosophy and read Greek, Muslim and other works on the subject. Ibn Sina later learnt logic, metaphysics and other subjects from a famous philosopher of the time, Abu Abdullah Natili.

However, he is soon said to have outgrown all his teachers. For the next few years, he busied himself with self-education. During this time, he also mastered Islamic law and medicine, finding the latter "not difficult".

By the age of 18, he had attained such mastery in medicine that his fame spread far and wide. It was around this time that he was called upon to treat the Samanid ruler Noor Ibn Mansoor, the King of Bukhara, whom many well-known physicians were unable to cure. Ibn Sina succeeded and the grateful king was willing to give him any reward. All he sought, however, was permission to use the royal library, which was a treasure trove of rare manuscripts on various subjects.

When he turned 21, he had gone through many of the best books, absorbing their knowledge. He was now in a position to himself write a book, his first one. Around this time, he was given an administrative post and is even said to have served as a clerk.

Great Wanderings

His fortunes suddenly took a turn for the worse, though. First, his father died. Second, the Samanid ruler was defeated by Mahmud of Ghazni, the legendary Turkish conqueror who established his rule over large parts of Iran and Afghanistan, then called Khorasan. Leaving his native Bukhara, he began a life of wandering, going westwards across different cities of Khorasan. He served the King of Khiva, Ali ibn Ma'mun, for some time.

But faced with the fear of being kidnapped by Mahmud of Ghazni, he once again hit the dirt road. Many great wanderings later, he reached Jurjan, near the Caspian Sea. The Jurjan ruler was famed as a patron of learning and he hoped to find refuge here. However, shortly after Ibn Sina's arrival, Jurjan's ruler was deposed and murdered. For some time, he stayed here, lecturing on logic and astronomy and also writing the first part of the *Qanun fi al-Tibb*, his greatest work, which was known in the West as the *Canon.*

Later, Ibn Sina moved to Rayy (near present-day Tehran) and thence to Qazvin. As was his wont, he earned his keep as a physician. Yet, he was unable to find his bearings or adequate support in these cities, either to live peacefully or to continue his work. So he travelled to Hamadan in west-central Persia, which was ruled by Shams ad-Daulah. Hamadan's ruler was then suffering from a severe case of colic and Ibn Sina treated him successfully.

He was appointed court physician and finding royal favour was thereafter appointed wazir. This did not go down well with some people and there were court intrigues against him. Although he went into hiding temporarily, he was imprisoned for some time. Fortunately for him, Shams ad-Daulah again fell prey to colic and called him back, reinstating him as wazir!

Medical Masterpieces

At this point of time, his busy practice during the day meant he had to spend long hours at night lecturing his students and dictating notes for his books. It was now that he began working on *Kitab ash-Shifa* (*The Book of Healing*). A vast philosophical and scientific encyclopaedia, it is said to be the largest work of its kind ever written by one man. Even during periods of confinement, he would continue to write. The book covers logic, psychology, the natural sciences, geometry, arithmetic, astronomy, music and metaphysics. In large measure, Aristotle and other Greek masters influenced his thoughts and beliefs in this treatise. The common thread in this work is the essence and existence of God.

The other work he was composing at this time was the *Qanun fi al-Tibb* (*The Canon of Medicine*), the most famous book on medicine in the East or West. A medical encyclopaedia that was over a million words long, this masterpiece was based primarily on the works of Greek and Arab physicians and, to some extent, on his own clinical experiences, although his notes were lost during constant wanderings. The book described over 760 drugs and was rated the best *materia medica* of its time. His work made major contributions in anatomy, gynaecology and child health. He was also the first physician to describe meningitis.

On the death of Shams ad-Daulah in 1022 AD, his life once again plunged into turmoil. He was imprisoned for a while, but later managed to flee to Isfahan, which lay 250 miles south of Tehran. For the next 14 years, he was able to live in relative peace, completing his two major works. He also wrote most of his treatises in Isfahan. He spent these years in the service of Isfahan's ruler, Ala ad-Daulah. He advised the king on scientific and literary matters and even accompanied him on military campaigns.

Bold Treatises

During this period, he wrote his last major philosophical work, *Kitab al-Isharat wa at-Tanbihat* (*The Book of Directives and Remarks*). Here, he described the spiritual journey of the mystic from the beginning of faith to the final stage of a direct vision of God.

Through his works, he managed to achieve a systematic integration of Greek rationalism and Islamic thought. Yet, in the process he sidelined several orthodox religious tenets, including the belief in the immortality of the soul and in the creation of the world. Orthodox Islamic thinkers, including the noted theologian al-Ghazali, later attacked his beliefs vehemently. Furthermore, Ibn Sina dared to claim that religion was nothing but philosophy in a metaphorical form that catered to the masses, since philosophical truths as rational formulations were beyond their comprehension.

Before Ibn Sina bade adieu to this world, he wrote 99 books, most of which were in Arabic, the prevalent language in the Muslim world of that era. He wrote two of these works in Farsi, his native tongue. One was the *Danish-naama-i-Alai* (*Encyclopaedia of Philosophical Sciences*) and a small treatise on the pulse. Of his books, 68 were on theology and metaphysics, 16 on medicine, 11 on astronomy and four on verse. His most celebrated poem in Arabic is a description of the descent of the soul into the body from the heavens.

Ibn Sina's constant travelling and non-stop work and writing told on his health. Despite the advice of friends, he stuck to his hectic work schedule. On one of his campaigns with Ala ad-Daulah, he fell ill. Despite his attempts to treat himself, he succumbed to colic and exhaustion in the city of Hamadan in 1037 AD. He was only 58. His grave can still be seen in Hamadan.

❑ ❑ ❑

AL-GHAZALI (1058–1111 AD)

The Sufi Mystic

A Muslim theologian, mystic and philosopher, al-Ghazali was born at Tus, Persia (near Mashad in eastern Iran) in 1058 AD. His full name was Abu Hamid Muhammad Ibn Muhammad At-tusi al-Ghazali. His father died when he was young.

However, his guardians ensured he had excellent education. Al-Ghazali was first educated at Tus, then in Jorjan and finally at Nishapur, where he learned under a renowned theologian of that time, al-Juwayni.

Thanks to his intellectual prowess, at the early age of 33, the Abbasid wazir, Nizam al-Mulk appointed him a professor at the Nizamiya University in Baghdad, which was rated as one of the most reputed institutions of learning in the Muslim world. Al-Ghazali was greatly influenced by Greek philosophy.

In his corpus of over 40 works, al-Ghazali penned numerous treatises that attempted to refute the doctrines of the Ismailis. The most detailed of these works is the *Fada'ih al-Batiniyya wa fada'il al-Mustazhiriyya* (*The Infamies of the Batiniyya and the Virtues of the Mustazhiriyya*), more commonly referred to as the *Kitab al-Mustazhiri.*

Years after he became a professor in Baghdad, he was beset by intense intellectual scepticism, which was an outcome of his deep philosophical studies. Since his sceptical queries had no answers, he felt a religious storm consume his being, where the question of his eternal destiny kept haunting him.

This embattled state of mind led to the rise of psychosomatic symptoms, forcing him to quit his professorship. Leaving his family too, he decided to devote his life to seeking the path to paradise. The *Kitab al-Mustazhiri* was probably the last composition before the personal crisis that forced his departure from Baghdad towards the end of 1095 AD.

Mystical Transformation

Taking to the life of a wandering ascetic, he sought the truth in Sufi mysticism. During these years as an ascetic, he underwent a mystical transformation. He learned that there were states of higher consciousness above and beyond the senses and the intellect. It was in such a state of the highest consciousness that one could directly experience God. Through his own personal experience, Ghazali realised that this was the same state the prophets were in when they received Divine revelations. Once he himself underwent this experience, all his questions were answered. He was himself the recipient of the Ultimate Truth.

Eleven years later, he returned to his teaching activities. This time, though, he was a devoted religious philosopher who had found the truth through Islamic Sufism. The rest of his life was dedicated to Sufi ideals.

A prolific writer, some of his other noteworthy works include *al-Munqidh min ad-Dalal* (*The Deliverance from Error*), *Bidayat al-Hidayah* (*The Beginning of Guidance*), *Tuhafut al-Falasifa* (*The Incoherence of Philosophers*) and *Ihya 'Ulum ad-Din* (*The Revival of the Religious Sciences*).

The *al-Munqidh min ad-Dalal* describes his internal struggle, the intellectual development and the religious deliverance through his journey to Sufi mysticism. With the most details about his life, this book is akin to an autobiography and has been compared in Western circles with *The Confessions of Saint Augustine. Bidayat al-Hidayah* has practical instructions for a Muslim who desires to follow the path to Sufi mysticism.

Having gained an element of mastery over philosophy, Ghazali wrote *Tuhafut al-Falasifa* – a scathing indictment of speculative Islamic theology and Greek philosophy (*Falasifa*). The attack was specifically against the Neoplatonic theories of Muslim philosophers such as Ibn Sina (Avicenna), which were opposed to orthodox theological doctrines like that of the Creation and the immortality of the soul.

Ihya 'Ulum ad-Din presents his composite view of religion that incorporates elements from three supposedly contradictory sources: tradition, intellectualism and mysticism. Many consider this work the greatest religious book in the Islamic world, next only to the *Koran.*

He also wrote a summary of astronomy. During the Middle Ages, some of his works were translated into European languages, attesting to the influence of his thoughts.

The Incomprehensible Absolute

In his philosophical treatises, Ghazali spoke of the inability of reason to comprehend the Absolute and the Infinite. Reason, he stressed, could never transcend the finite and was limited to the observation of the relative. And contradicting several Muslim philosophers, who believed that the universe was finite in space but infinite in time, he held that the universe was infinite in space as well as time.

His logic created a balance between religion and reason, with religion being identified with the infinite and reason with the finite. His approach is said to have benefited both Sufism and orthodox Islam. He rid Sufism of its elements of excesses, such as the avoidance of obligatory prayers, re-establishing the authority of the orthodox religion. But he stressed that genuine Sufism was the right path to attain the Absolute Truth.

Before his death on December 18, 1111 AD in his hometown Tus, Ghazali came to be regarded as an expert in all three major disciplines of eleventh-century Muslim thought – *islam* (practice), *iman* (doctrine), and *ihsan* (realisation). Which is why many still consider him as the greatest Muslim philosopher of that era. Thanks to his efforts, Sufism (once regarded as a secret society) became an acceptable part of orthodox Islam.

❑ ❑ ❑

IBN RUSHD (1126–1198)

The Commentator

One of the foremost Islamic thinkers, Ibn Rushd's full name was Abû al-Walîd Muhammad ibn Ahmad ibn Muhammad ibn Rushd. He integrated Greek philosophy, particularly Aristotle's teachings, and Islamic traditions into a school of thought of his own.

Popularly known as Averroës in Spain and the West, this Spanish-Arab philosopher, jurist and physician was born in 1126 in Cordoba, Spain, where his father was a judge, as had been his grandfather. It was his father who instructed him in Muslim jurisprudence. He also studied theology, philosophy and mathematics under the Arab philosopher Ibn Tufayl (1105–85) and medicine under the Arab physician Avenzoar.

Being fully conversant with the traditional Muslim sciences (particularly the Islamic Scripture or *Koran*, the Traditions or *Hadith* and the Law or *Fiqh*), he was appointed *qazi* or judge in Seville (1169) and rose to the post of chief *qazi* in Cordoba (1171). After the death of the Arab philosopher Ibn Tufayl in 1182, Averroës succeeded him as chief physician to Abu Yaqub Yusuf, the Almohad caliph of Morocco and Muslim Spain and to his son, Abu Yusuf Yaqub, in 1184.

It was Ibn Tufayl who had first introduced Averroës to the caliph, Abu Yaqub, in 1169. The caliph was himself a keen student of philosophy and unnerved Averroës by asking him whether the heavens were created or not. Sensing his discomfiture, the caliph answered the question himself! Thereafter, a long conversation followed. When Averroës left, he had been plied with expensive gifts.

Rediscovering Aristotle

This meeting had an important influence on his life, as not long afterwards, the caliph asked Averroës to provide a correct interpretation of Aristotle's philosophy. Despite his busy schedule as a judge, he got down to the task in right earnest between 1169 and 1195. He penned a series of commentaries on most of Aristotle's works including the *Organon*, *Rhetorica*, *Poetica*, *De Anima*, *De Partibus Animalium*, *Physica*, *Metaphysica*, *Parva Naturalia*, *Meteorologica* and *Nicomachean Ethics*. These extensive commentaries exercised a great influence over Jewish and Christian writers for centuries, after they were translated into Latin and Hebrew, leading to a rediscovery of Aristotle's work after these had been in near-oblivion for centuries.

Averroës' commentaries on Aristotle's treatises on natural sciences are a tribute to his penetrative insight and power of observation. Thanks to Averroës' clear observations, people were better able to understand the ancient Greek philosopher.

The first work all his own was *Kulliyat* (*General Medicine* or *Colliget* in Latin), which was written between 1162 and 1169. Between 1179 and 1180, he also composed three religious-philosophical polemical treatises – *Fasl* (the *Decisive Treatise on the Agreement Between Religious Law and Philosophy*), an Appendix to the *Fasl* called *Manahij* (*Appendix: Examination of the Methods of Proof Concerning the Doctrines of Religions*), and *Tuhafut al-Tuhafut* (*The Incoherence of the Incoherence*), which was a staunch defence of philosophy. In *The Incoherence of the Incoherence*, he rebutted Islamic thinker and theologian al-Ghazali's attack on

Neoplatonic and Aristotelian philosophy and on Ibn Sina in particular, accusing Ghazali of making inconsistent arguments.

In his first two works, he made the bold claim that only the metaphysician using specific proof was capable and competent enough to interpret the doctrines contained in the *Shariah* (the Islamic law that was revealed prophetically). The Muslim *mutakallimun* (dialetic theologians) were not qualified to do this, he claimed, as they simply relied on dialectic arguments. The aim of philosophy, he stressed, was to reveal the true, inner meaning of religious beliefs and thereby come to the Truth. However, this Ultimate Truth could not be divulged to the masses since it surpasses human understanding and the common people must be taught the truth through stories, similes or metaphors.

Like al-Farabi and Plato had held much before his time, Averroës envisaged a state where philosophers would be counted as the elite. But since the ideal Muslim state also provided for the happiness of the masses (unlike Plato's ideal state) and its law having been revealed prophetically, he held it was superior to the Greek *nomos* (law). He, however, regretted the unequal position of women in Islam, compared to the equality in Plato's *Republic*. He opined that considering women fit only for childbearing and rearing was not in the best interests of the state and its economic prosperity – an extremely brave stance in that era, indeed.

Averroës felt that if both philosophy and Islam were properly understood, there was no incompatibility between the two and the layman could be taught the Truth through traditions and the *Koran*, without trying to turn the layperson into a philosopher. Despite his sound arguments, the atmosphere in Muslim Spain and North Africa was not conducive to such philosophical speculation, as philosophy was considered anti-Islamic and philosophers were viewed with extreme suspicion.

In 1195, he suddenly fell into disfavour with Abu Yusuf, when a *jihad* (holy war) was launched against Christian Spain. Averroës was dismissed from office and banished to Lucena. This was most likely an attempt by the caliph to appease the theologians and ensure the support of the masses during the *jihad.* During this period, many of his works on logic and metaphysics were consigned to the flames, much to his acute distress.

This banishment was short-lived, as the caliph recalled the philosopher soon. Despite this temporary aberration, there is no doubt that without the caliph's support it would have been well-nigh impossible for Averroës to have pursued his philosophical vocation. The philosopher admitted this by dedicating his *Commentary on Plato's Republic* to the ruler.

The Double Truth

Although Averroës never said so himself, Christian thinkers later interpreted his works as propounding a "double truth" – philosophical and religious. It is possible that Latin Averroists formulated the theory of the "double truth". Averroës' works make it clear that he believed in only one truth – that of the religious law, which he said was the same truth philosophers were seeking. He stated clearly that religious teachings about reward and punishment and the Hereafter must be accepted completely by all classes of people.

Rejecting the belief that the universe was created during the history of time, he said the universe has no beginning. God is the "prime mover", he stressed, the self-moved force that stimulates all motion, transforming the potential into the actual. The individual human soul was nothing but an emanation of the Universal Soul.

After he was recalled by the caliph and returned to Marrakesh, Averroës spent his last days here, where he died in 1198. He was first buried at Marrakesh, but his mortal remains were later shifted to the family tomb at Cordoba. Besides his books on metaphysics, this great Islamic thinker also wrote on medicine, astronomy, law and grammar. A tribute to his influence was the fact that 'Averroism' was taught at Paris and other places in the 13th century, by Averroists who distinguished philosophical truth from revealed religion.

JALAL UD-DIN RUMI (1207–1273)

Dance of the Divine

Poet, philosopher and mystic of Islam, Rumi was the founder of the Mevlavi Sufi order, a leading mystical brotherhood of Islam. Rumi was born in a family of theologians on September 30, 1207 at Balkh in the north-eastern province of Persia, which is in present-day Afghanistan. His full name was Maulana Jalal ud-Din Mohammad Ibn Husain al-Rumi. His father, Baha ud-Din, was a renowned religious scholar from whom Rumi received his early theological education.

When Rumi was five years old, the family left his birthplace and went to Baghdad. Three years later, they left this city too and moved to Mecca, performing the Haj. Thereafter, they went to Damascus and finally to Malatia (in Western Euphrates, Turkey). Having spent over a decade in various cities, around 1226 AD the family finally settled at Konya in the north-western provinces of Persia (present-day Turkey), which was then part of the Seljuk Empire and its capital city. The family's early migrations were prompted to escape the death and destruction wrought by the invading Mongol hordes.

Around this time, at the age of 19, Rumi was married to Gevher Khatun. When Rumi was 24, his father died in 1231 and he succeeded him as a professor of religious sciences at the renowned madrasa in Konya. After his father's death, Syed Burhan ud-Din, a friend of his father, took over his spiritual education. For the next nine years, he instructed Rumi in "the science of prophets and states". He also instructed Rumi on the strict 40-day retreat and included other disciplines like meditation and fasting.

By this time, Rumi was already considered an accomplished scholar in religious and positive sciences. At the age of 25, Rumi went to Aleppo for advanced education. Later, he would go to Damascus for further education. He spent the next four years interacting with some of the greatest religious minds of the era. It was through Syed Burhan ud-Din that Rumi received his first mystical training.

The Dervish and the Mystic

With each passing year, Rumi's knowledge and consciousness of God increased by leaps and bounds. Finally, Syed Burhan ud-Din felt he had fulfilled his responsibility in teaching his friend's son and returned to his hometown. Before leaving, however, he told Rumi a great friend would come to him, who would lead him to "the innermost parts of the spiritual world, just as you will lead him". The two would complement each other, Syed Burhan ud-Din foretold.

And so it came to pass. On November 28, 1244 AD, Rumi and the wandering dervish Shams ud-Din Tabriz met for the first time. Later, Rumi would say about this meeting: "What I had thought of before as God, I met today in person." Before this meeting, Rumi had been an eminent professor of religion and an acclaimed mystic. After this, he became an inspired poet suffused with a great love for humanity.

Their companionship was comparatively brief. On March 14, 1246, Shams left Rumi for the first time. Rumi's son, Sultan Valed, managed to track Shams down in Damascus and the two were reunited. Some time later in 1247, Shams disappeared again, never to be seen thereafter. The grief-stricken Rumi composed nearly 30,000 verses on the loss of his soul mate. It was generally believed that those who resented his proximity to Rumi might have murdered Shams.

The Spiritual Couplets

Nearly a decade after first meeting Shams, Rumi was still composing spontaneous *ghazals* (odes), which were put down in a large volume called *Divan-i-Kabir.* During this time, Rumi had developed a deep spiritual bonding with Husamuddin Chelebi. One day, Husamuddin requested Rumi to write a book from which people could "fill their hearts". Rumi smiled and from under the folds of his turban drew a piece of paper, which contained the opening 18 lines of his work, *Masnavi-ye Manavi* (*Spiritual Couplets*), beginning with:

> *Listen to the reed and the tale it tells,*
> *How it sings of separation...*

Husamuddin wept tears of joy, begging Rumi to write more volumes. Rumi replied: "Chelebi, if you consent to write for me, I will recite."

Thereafter, Rumi began dictating his monumental work. Husamuddin later recalled: "He never took a pen in his hand while composing the *Masnavi.* Wherever he happened to be, whether in the school, at the Ilgin hot springs, in the Konya baths, or in the Meram vineyards, I would write down what he recited. Often I could barely keep up with his pace, sometimes night and day for several days. At other times, he would not compose for months and once, for two years there was nothing. At the completion of each book I would read it back to him, so that he could correct what had been written."

Many consider the *Masnavi-ye Manavi* the greatest spiritual treatise ever written, spanning seven volumes and 24,660 couplets, the majority in Farsi (his mother tongue) and some in Arabic. With love as its basic theme, the book deals with the problems and speculations that impact the conduct, meaning and purpose of life and the perennial longing of the human soul for union with God. The largest mystical exposition in verse, the book expounds on metaphysics, ethics, religion, culture, politics, sex, domestic issues and mysticism. The *Masnavi* immensely influenced Islamic literature and thought. It also has detailed expositions on the natural world, history and geography.

He also wrote *Divan-e-Shams* (a compendium of poems in praise of Shams that run to over 45,000 verses in Farsi) and *Fihi-Ma-Fihi* (a collection of mystical sayings).

The Whirling Dervishes

The greatest Sufi mystic and philosopher, Rumi passed away at sunset on December 17, 1273 AD at Konya. Men of five faiths are said to have followed his bier. The great man was laid to rest beside his father. Over his mortal remains, the splendid 13th century Mevlana Mausoleum still stands. With a mosque, dance hall, dervish living quarters, school and tombs of some teachers of the Mevlavi Order, the shrine draws pilgrims of all denominations from the world over.

The Mevlavi Order of Dervishes that Rumi founded is today famous as the Whirling Dervishes of Sufism. The Sufi way to ecstasy and discovery of the Divine is perhaps the most unusual: swift, turning body movements, mental focus and the use of sound.

No longer a secret society as in the days of yore, the Dervishes now tour the globe allowing audiences worldwide the opportunity to view the ceremony of their sacred dances and music.

MODERN PHILOSOPHERS

RENÉ DESCARTES (1596–1650)

The Father of Modern Philosophy

One of the greatest thinkers in human history, the French philosopher, scientist and mathematician – sometimes called the Father of Modern Philosophy – Rene Descartes was born on March 31, 1596 at La Haye, Touraine, France, in the family of a minor nobleman. His father, Joachim Descartes, was a councillor in Brittany. The fourth child in the family, Rene's mother died in childbirth when he was a year old. Thereafter, his father remarried and Rene's grandmother probably brought him up. When he was still a small boy, Rene wanted to know about "the reasons of things and their causes", which made his father refer to him as "my little philosopher".

Enrolled in the Jesuit school of La Flèche in Anjou when he was eight years old, he remained there for about ten years. One of the most famous schools of that era, he was taught Scholastic philosophy, mathematics and the usual classical studies. This early schooling ensured that Roman Catholicism would exert a strong influence on Descartes for the rest of his life.

Dream and Destiny

Having completed his schooling, he enrolled at the University of Poitiers to study law and graduated in 1616. However, he never practised law, as destiny had greater plans in store. Dabbling with a career in the military, he joined the service of Prince Maurice of Nassau at Breda, Netherlands, in 1618. Over the next few years, although he enlisted in other armies, including that of the Duke of Bavaria, this was not to be his professional calling. The realm of mathematics and philosophy had already caught his eye and he would devote the rest of his life in pursuit of these subjects.

It was on November 10, 1619 that he decided his mission in life would be to devote his time to restoring human knowledge. It was a dream that changed the course of his life. Interpreting the dream as a revelation, he was convinced "it was the Spirit of Truth that willed to open for him all the treasures of knowledge". For a man who operated purely by logic and reason, the revelation through a dream added a mystical element to his search, but one that he was totally convinced about.

Between 1623–24, he went on a pilgrimage, visiting Brittany, Poitou, Switzerland and Italy. In 1625, Descartes returned to Paris. He lived in France until 1628, devoting himself to philosophy on one hand, while also dabbling in optics. While studying optics, he discovered the fundamental law of refraction – the angle of incidence is equal to the angle of refraction – and wrote the first-ever essay on this topic. Indeed, Descartes is considered the founder of the science of optics.

However, Paris simply didn't offer him the peace, the quiet and the independence he sought to pursue his interests. The noise and bustle of city life was simply not to his liking and he yearned for "the innocence of the desert". Selling his properties in France, he shifted to the Netherlands in 1629. It was here that he lived the remainder of his life, spending time in different cities like Amsterdam, Deventer, Leiden and Utrecht, shifting to as many as 18 different locations.

It was from his Dutch retreats that Descartes wrote treatises like *Essais Philosophiques* (1637), *Meditationes de Prima Philosophia* (*Meditations on the First Philosophy*, 1641), *Principia Philosophia* (*Principles of Philosophy*, 1644) and *Treatise on the Passions* (1649). He dedicated *Principia Philosophia* to Princess Elizabeth of Bohemia, with whom he had developed a deep friendship after they met in 1643 and who was then living in exile in the Netherlands. *Essais Philosophiques* had four parts: an essay on geometry, a second on optics, a third on meteors and the fourth, *Discours de la Methode* (*Discourse on Method*), which dwelt on his philosophical speculations and was the most famous of his works.

Cartesianism

He had finished another important work, *Le Monde* (*The World*) in 1633, but put off its publication after the Church in Rome condemned Galileo to death for heresy, as he had advocated the Copernican system. Reading Galileo's work, Descartes realised he subscribed to some similar beliefs, including the theory that the earth moved around the sun. A devout Catholic, and a man who loved peace and quiet, confrontation with the Church was the last thing he would risk, so he dropped the idea of publishing *Le Monde.*

His approach to science, sometimes referred to as Cartesianism, was based on elaborate but sometimes erroneous explanations of physical phenomena. In mathematics, he made a significant contribution through his systematisation of analytic geometry. In philosophy, he applied the rational inductive methods of science and mathematics, rejecting the Scholastic method of comparing and contrasting the views of recognised authorities.

Commenting on this approach, Descartes said: "In our search for the direct road to truth, we should busy ourselves with no object about which we cannot attain a certitude equal to that of the demonstration of arithmetic and geometry." Until he had solid proof of something being true, he refused to believe in it and applied this yardstick even to his own existence! The very fact that he could doubt his very existence, however, was proof enough that he existed!

This gave rise to his famous statement: *Cogito, ergo sum* ("I think, therefore I am"). Based on the premise that the consciousness of his thinking was proof of his own existence, he went on to argue the existence of God. The very idea of God implied the existence of God, he opined, simply because a finite or imperfect being like man could never have thought of the idea of an infinite or perfect being such as God. This was only possible if God had revealed this to man.

Cartesian Dualism

Despite his rational and mechanistic ways, he accepted the theological doctrine about the immortality of the soul, but held that the mind and the body were two distinct substances. This freed the mind from the mechanistic laws of nature, allowing it the freedom of will. Simply put, he said God had created two kinds of substances that comprise the entire universe: one with thinking substances or minds and the other with extended substances or bodies. This separation of the mind and body was referred to as Cartesian Dualism. It was this doctrine that saved him from direct confrontation with the Church. Critics inquired, however, as to how it was possible that two different substances such as the mind and body could affect each other; the conundrum still remains unresolved.

Descartes believed that God created the universe and everything therein depended on God's grace. God, in his opinion, was like the human mind – thinking and existing, but without physical attributes. Unlike the human mind, though, which is finite, God is infinite and without a creator.

In *Meditations*, he pushed his methodological doubt further, through the hypothesis of an omnipotent and malicious demon who could make everything that one thinks exists into no more than a great cosmic deception. Yet, the person who is deceived exists. The very fact of his deception proves his existence!

The kind of theological semantics contained in *Meditations* attracted renown and controversy. The president of the University of Utrecht in Holland accused Descartes of atheism. It was not long before his former Jesuit teachers in France also rejected Cartesianism. His works were thereafter put on the *Index*, a list of books forbidden by the Catholic Church.

When his 1649 book, *Passions*, was published, Queen Christina of Sweden had received a copy through the French ambassador. In fact, she had been receiving copies of his works since 1647 and evinced a keen interest in meeting the philosopher. After putting off her invitation more than once, Descartes finally travelled to Stockholm in October 1649. His prime task was to instruct the 23-year-old queen in philosophy.

Unfortunately, he had to tutor her at 5:00 every morning. In Sweden's harsh climate – where "men's thoughts freeze during the winter months", in Descartes' words – this was too much for a man who had a frail childhood. He caught a chill that quickly developed into pneumonia.

After receiving the last sacraments, he died on February 11, 1650.

IMMANUEL KANT (1724–1804)

The Philosophy of Transcendentalism

The German philosopher Immanuel Kant – considered one of the foremost thinkers of the modern era – was born at Königsberg in East Prussia (now in Russia) on April 22, 1724. He was educated at the Collegium Fredericianum and the University of Königsberg. In college, he studied the classics. At the university, it was physics and mathematics. Through his teacher, Martin Knutzen, he learnt about the philosophy of Wolff and of Newton's physics.

After his father's death in 1746, he had to quit his career at the university due to financial constraints. For the next nine years, he earned his living as a private tutor. Thanks to the help provided by a friend, in 1755 he returned to Königsberg and resumed his studies, later securing a doctorate. He then taught at the university for the next 15 years. In the beginning, he lectured only on science and mathematics. Later, he enlarged his field by teaching almost all branches of philosophy.

Between 1755 and 1770, he was a *Privatdozent* (unsalaried professor) at the university. During this period, his lectures and works helped him make a mark as an original philosopher. He was only appointed professor of logic and metaphysics in

1770. He then held this position at the university for the next 27 years.

Initially, Leibnitz and Wolff influenced Kant. Later, he read the works of David Hume and English empiricists. Over the coming years, Kant developed his own critical philosophy in which he dwelt upon the nature and limits of human knowledge, the principles of the mind and consciousness, and their ethical and aesthetic results.

Analytic and Synthetic

The main tenets of Kant's philosophy were published in his treatise, *Critique of Pure Reason* (1781), in which he examined the basis of human knowledge. Kant held that there were two modes of thinking, analytic and synthetic. Analytical propositions are self-evident and the truth is obvious in the statement itself. Consider the statement: "Black panthers are panthers." The truth about this statement is self-evident, since the reverse of this statement could not be true. On the other hand, synthetic propositions are those that cannot be deduced from pure analysis. For instance, "The panther is black." Propositions based on experiences of the world are synthetic.

Furthermore, propositions could be divided into two categories: empirical and *a priori.* The former depend purely on the perception of the senses, while the latter are fundamentally valid and not dependent on sense perceptions. "The panther is black" is an empirical statement, while "two plus two is four" is a *priori.* Kant held that one could make synthetic *a priori* judgements, a philosophical stand known as transcendentalism. This was possible, Kant observed, because the objects of our material universe are fundamentally unknowable. Like space and time, objects per se have no existence and merely exist as part of the mind, "intuitions" by which perceptions are measured.

Furthermore, Kant held that the mind allows archetypal forms and categories (time, space and substance) to its sensations. But logically, these categories come prior to the experience, although they are manifest only in experience. These categories or structural principles being prior to experience, they are transcendental in nature. That is, they transcend all experience, whether actual or possible. While these principles determine all experience, they do not themselves affect the nature of things in any manner.

Therefore, the knowledge of those things, for which these principles are prerequisites, must not be thought of as revelations of the things themselves. This knowledge holds good for things only to the extent that they appear so to human perception or can be apprehended by the senses.

Therefore, Kant argued, *the framework of experience limited human knowledge and the human mind was incapable of going beyond experience into the realm of Ultimate Reality strictly on the basis of knowledge.* This was the essence of Kant's philosophy, outlined in three major treatises, *Critique of Pure Reason* (1781), *Critique of Practical Reason* (1788), and *Critique of Judgement* (1790).

In all these works, Kant attempted to bridge the dichotomy between science and religion by propounding that the world existed at two levels: (i) *noumena*, comprising objects conceived by reason although these were imperceptible to the senses, (ii) *phenomena*, comprising objects as they appear to the senses and are accessible to physical study. Which is why, he said that the soul and God were noumenal realities and could only be understood through faith and not by scientific study.

Kant's philosophy of transcendentalism was an amalgam of several viewpoints. It is agnostic in that it claimed a strict knowledge of Ultimate Reality or God is not possible. It is empirical, since it says that all knowledge comes from experience and holds true for objects of actual and potential experience. It is also rationalistic, as it maintains the *a priori* character of the structural principles of this empirical knowledge.

Over the years, Kant's unorthodox religious teachings courted considerable controversy, primarily because they were based on rational thought rather than revelations. His beliefs upset the Prussian Government and in 1792, the King of Prussia,

Frederick William II, forbade him from teaching or writing on religious topics.

For the next five years, Kant heeded the ban, until the king died, whereupon he took to propagating his views once again.

Other Works

Besides philosophy, Kant wrote treatises on other subjects. An important scientific treatise was *General Natural History and Theory of the Heavens* (1755). Here, he theorised that the universe was formed from a spinning nebula. Subsequently, Pierre de Laplace also independently developed a similar hypothesis. The other writings included *Prolegomena to Any Future Metaphysics* (1783), *Metaphysical Rudiments of Natural Philosophy* (1786), *Critique of Judgment* (1790), and *Religion Within the Boundaries of Pure Reason* (1793).

Then followed the *Metaphysics of Ethics* (1797), in which Kant described his ethical system, based on the belief that reason is the final authority for morality. In *Critique of Practical Reason* (1788), he put down his beliefs in the fundamental freedom of the individual. This freedom, however, was not to be confused with the lawless freedom of anarchy. Instead, it was the freedom of self-government and the freedom to consciously obey the laws of the universe based upon reason. In *Perpetual Peace* (1795), he put forth the idea of a global federation of republican states. It was the philosophical principles of Kant that heavily influenced a later German philosopher, Georg Hegel, and subsequently Karl Marx, giving birth to Marxism.

In 1797, Kant retired from the University of Königsberg. A year later, he published a summary of his religious views. On February 12, 1804 one of the most influential German philosophers of all time passed away, leaving an indelible mark that would heavily influence philosophers of coming generations.

❑ ❑ ❑

GEORG W.F. HEGEL (1770–1831)

The German Idealist

One of the foremost German philosophers, Georg Wilhelm Friedrich Hegel's views widely influenced other thinkers in Germany and elsewhere. The son of a revenue officer in the civil service, Hegel was born on August 27, 1770 in Stuttgart.

Having been taught elementary Latin by his mother, he was enrolled in the Stuttgart grammar school and remained there till the age of 18.

Brought up in the atmosphere of Protestant orthodoxy, he was fully acquainted with the Greek and Roman classics. As per the wishes of his parents, in 1788 he entered the seminary at the University of Tübingen. It was here that he developed friendships with the poet Friedrich Hölderlin and the philosopher Friedrich Wilhelm Joseph von Schelling, who was junior to him by five years. He studied philosophy and the classics for two years and graduated in 1790.

Hegel then took the theological course but, before long, the orthodoxy of his teachers made him restless. He changed his mind and decided not to enter the ministry, leaving in 1793. Wanting to have sufficient time to pursue philosophy and Greek literature, he became a private tutor in Berne, Switzerland. He lived here for the next three years. It was during these years that he acquainted himself well with the Greek and Roman classics.

Kantian Influence and After

Around this time, Hegel also read the works of the philosopher Immanuel Kant and was deeply influenced by them. Later, under the Kantian influence, Hegel began to reinterpret the Gospel and tried answering the question about how Christianity turned into an authoritarian religion it then was, when the teachings of Jesus Christ were rational, not authoritarian. His attacks were never against theology itself, but purely against orthodoxy.

In 1796, Hegel moved to Frankfurt and later began giving private tuitions. In the coming years, Hegel gradually emerged from the shadow of Kantian influence, being inspired by the doctrine of the Holy Spirit. The spirit of man, Hegel believed, is the candle of the Lord and couldn't be constrained in the way that Kant sought to portray. All his works therefore had the outlook of a historian, unlike Kant, who veered towards physical science.

A couple of years later, Hegel had a second look at the essays he had penned swayed by Kant's thoughts. He realised that under Kant's influence he had misinterpreted the teachings of Christ and the history of the Church. These reformed thoughts he expressed in his essay, *Der Geist des Christentums und sein Schicksal* (*The Spirit of Christianity and Its Fate*), which was only published in 1907 and is considered one of his best works.

At times difficult to comprehend, it nevertheless has an undercurrent of passion and conviction. Kant had opined that man was capable of knowing only the finite world of appearances and trying to go beyond this to understand the Infinite or Ultimate Reality only led to unresolved contradictions. Hegel held otherwise, however, saying that through the medium of love contradictions like the Infinite and the finite were synthesised. The word *Geist* used in the title of his essay had religious connotations, as it meant 'spirit' as well as 'mind'.

Hegel's father expired in 1799, which meant a financial legacy that, though not substantial, helped free him from the clutches of tutoring to earn his keep. He was now free to fulfil his ambition of an academic career. Enrolling at the University of Jena in January 1801, he studied here and eventually became a lecturer. It was here that the precocious nature philosopher Schelling, who already had a few books under his belt, was a professor since 1798. In 1801–02, Hegel gave lectures on logic and metaphysics. Schelling left Jena in 1803, which meant Hegel could work without being unduly influenced by another philosopher.

Yet, the influence of Greek philosophers is clear in his work. Other philosophers he read were Baruch Spinoza, the Dutch philosopher; Jean Jacques Rousseau, the French writer; and the German philosophers of the era.

In February 1805, Hegel was appointed extraordinary professor at Jena. Thanks to the intervention of Goethe, Hegel received a stipend for the first time in 1806, which was all of 100 thalers.

In October of that year, however, Hegel was forced to flee Jena when the city fell to the French. By this time, he had already spent his father's legacy. The reverses forced him to take up a job as the editor of the *Bamberger Zeitung*, in Bavaria, between 1807 and 1808.

The Absolute Spirit

His first great work, *Phanomenologie des Geistes* (*The Phenomenology of Mind*) was published in 1807. Although difficult to comprehend, the book is a brilliant description of man's mind rising from mere consciousness to self-consciousness, reason, spirit and religion and, finally, to absolute knowledge.

Having no stomach for journalism, he then moved to Nuremberg and was the headmaster of a gymnasium between December 1808 and August 1816. Although the income wasn't very much, it was more than sufficient to keep the home fires burning. It was in Nuremberg that he married Marie von

Tucher, who was 22 years younger to him. They had three children, a daughter, who died soon after birth and two sons, Karl (1813) and Immanuel (1814). Hegel had also fathered an illegitimate boy Ludwig (1807), when he was at Jena, who later came to live with the Hegels.

Over a period of four years at Nuremberg, Hegel published *The Science of Logic* (1812, 1813, 1816). This work was to fetch him offers of professorships at Erlanger, Berlin and Heidelberg. He accepted the offer from the University of Heidelberg. In 1817, he published a systematic exposition of his entire philosophy, *Encyclopaedia of the Philosophical Sciences in Outline.* Based on faith, this work was an attempt to comprehend the entire universe as a systematic whole.

The *Encyclopaedia* was divided into three parts: Logic, Nature and Mind. In Logic, Hegel says that if man attempts to comprehend the notion of Pure Being, he discovers it is Emptiness or Nothing. Yet, Nothing actually *exists.* Despite being a contradiction, both exist together. Nature happens to be the opposite of spirit. Everything in nature exists in space and time. In Mind, the philosopher charts how the human mind developed from the subconscious to the conscious and then to rational will; thereafter, through human history as the embodiment of that will; finally, there is art, religion and philosophy, through which man ultimately realises he is a spirit, the spirit of God or what he called the Absolute Spirit.

In Hegel's view, philosophy had to chart the development of the Absolute Spirit. Hegel said the Absolute Spirit was nothing but Pure Thought or Mind in the process of self-development, the manifestations of which he traced through simple consciousness, through self-consciousness and, finally, the rise of reason.

Lectures for Posterity

In 1818, the University of Berlin renewed its offer for Hegel to teach philosophy. This time around, he accepted the offer. He was to remain in Berlin till the end. It was here that he published *The Philosophy of the Right* in 1821, his last full-length treatise. Thereafter, he devoted himself almost totally to his lectures. His published lectures include *The Philosophy of Fine Art* (1835–38), *Lectures on the History of Philosophy* (1833–36), *Lectures on the Philosophy of Religion* (1832), and *Lectures on the Philosophy of History* (1837).

By the time his end drew near, he was recognised as Germany's foremost philosopher. His students and followers were later to split into two camps, the right-wing and left-wing Hegelians. The right-wingers were politically orthodox and stressed compatibility between Christianity and his philosophy. The left-wingers eventually took an atheistic outlook and those into politics became revolutionaries. The left-wingers included Ludwig Feuerbach, Bruno Bauer, Friedrich Engels and Karl Marx, with the last two being the masterminds of Marxism, which was to alter much of world history by substituting Hegel's religious idealism with atheistic materialism.

On November 14, 1831 Hegel succumbed to a cholera epidemic.

❑ ❑ ❑

INDIAN PHILOSOPHERS

ADI SHANKARA (788–820 AD)

Poet, Philosopher and Mystic

Just as with many other aspects of his life, Adi Shankara's date of birth is disputed. It is likely that he was born in the year 788 AD. What is beyond dispute is that he was one of India's – and the world's – greatest poets, philosophers and mystics.

This great seer was born at a time when Buddhism was gaining ascendancy in India. Thanks to his irrefutable logic, he was able to swing the tide in favour of Hinduism.

Shankara was born to a learned Namboodiri Brahmin, Shivaguru and Aryaamba, in the backwater village of Kaladi in Kerala. The couple are said to have been childless for many years and received the child after they prayed at a temple in nearby Trichur, with legend having it that Shankara was an *avatar* of Lord Shiva. It is said that the Lord gave them the option of having one son who would be the most brilliant philosopher but short-lived or many mediocre sons. They chose the former.

Precocious and Brilliant

True to the legend, the child was precocious and brilliance personified. When he was barely three, his father died, leaving him to the tender care of his mother. Young Shankara is said to have excelled in all branches of traditional learning and also performed a few miracles.

Before long, he announced his wish to become a sannyasi, a wish his mother didn't accede to since he would be the only means of support in her old age.

This was not to be a stumbling block for long. One day, when Shankara and his mother were at the river having a bath, a crocodile is said to have seized him by the leg. He immediately called out to his mother, saying he had been seized by a crocodile and wished to take *apath-sannyasa* (the adoption of sannyas when death is near) immediately. Left with no choice, his mother quickly gave her consent, whereupon the crocodile immediately let go of his leg.

Although he took to sannyas, Shankara made one promise to his mother – on her death, he would return to perform her last rites.

Young Shankara then set out on a long journey to find a worthy guru who would initiate him into his fold. He reached the ashram of Swami Govindapada Acharya at Badrinath. Accepting him as a disciple, Govinda initiated him into the Paramahansa order, the highest renunciation. Swami Govinda taught Shankara all about the Advaita philosophy. Shankara was then commanded to spread this message by going to Kashi.

It was here that he began to write commentaries on the *Bhagavad Gita*, the *Upanishads* and the *Brahma Sutras*. He was barely 16.

Amongst Shankara's many works are: *Shareerik Bhasya*, *Brahma Sutras*, *Sanat Sujatiya*, *Sahasranama Adhyaya*, *Viveka Chudamani*, *Atma Bodha*, *Aparoksha Anubhuti*, *Ananda Lahari*, *Atma-Anatma Viveka* and *Upadesha Sahasn.*

Countrywide Debates

He now began travelling to all parts of the country, engaging other scholars and pundits in philosophical debates, as was the practice then. Whosoever was defeated was supposed to convert to the victor's philosophy. In this way, he defeated Bhatta Bhaskara, condemning his commentary on the *Vedanta Sutras*. Dandi, Mayura, Harsha, Abhinavagupta, Udayanacharya, Dharmagupta, Prabhakara and other philosophers of the era were also defeated.

That finally left the celebrated Kumarlila. When Shankara reached him, however, he was on his deathbed and asked the former to instead engage his disciple, Mandana Misra, in debate. Shankara duly went to Mandana Misra and challenged him to a religious debate. Misra agreed and Bharati, Misra's wife, was appointed the judge, since she was herself a very learned person. When Misra was duly defeated after more than a fortnight's debate, Bharati challenged Shankara to a debate, saying: "I am the other half of Mandana. You have defeated only one half of Mandana."

Realising that she couldn't defeat him in a debate, Bharati resorted to the science of *Kama Shastra*, about which Shankara, a celibate, didn't know anything. Not to be outdone, Shankara asked Bharati to give him a month's time to debate this topic with her.

Using his yogic powers, he left his physical body and made his astral body enter the body of a king, Raja Amaruka, who had just died and was about to be cremated. Naturally, the king arose from death to the astonishment of his people. For the next one month, through the king's body, Shankara learnt everything about *Kama Shastra*. He then returned to defeat Bharati.

Defying Religious Customs

News reached Shankara that his mother lay dying. Leaving his disciples, he proceeded quickly to Kaladi alone. After she passed away, he readied to perform her last rites, but was opposed by his relatives and the city's Namboodiri Brahmins, as a sannyasi was not allowed to perform such rites, having renounced family life. Defying narrow religious norms, Shankara is said to have cremated his mother's body in the backyard of his house.

Having fulfilled the vow to his mother, he returned to Sringeri. Thereafter, he left on a tour of the eastern coast, preaching the Advaita philosophy along the way. Shankara organised ten orders of sannyasis called 'Dasanamis'. He also established four mathas: Sringeri Matha, Dwarka Matha, Joshi Matha and Govardhana Matha.

Although he was never defeated in debate, a Chandala (untouchable) once left Shankara speechless. It so happened that Shankara was going for a bath in the Ganges when a Chandala happened to be in the way, along with his dogs. Shankara's disciples shouted at the man to get out of the way. Whereupon, the Chandala asked how a great preacher of Advaita Vedanta was making a distinction between himself and another man. And did Shankara want his transient physical body to move out of the way or his Self, the imperishable Atman?

Realising the deep significance of his probing query, Shankara prostrated before the untouchable, accepting him as his guru.

Brahman and the Unreal World

An adherent of Advaita Vedanta, Shankara believed there was only one Truth, the supreme Brahman, which was *Nirguna* (without qualities), *Nirakara* (formless), *Nirvivesha* (without attributes) and *Akarta* (non-agent).

According to Shankara: "This Atman is self-evident. This Atman or Self is not established by proofs of the existence of the Self. It is not possible to deny this Atman, for it is the very essence of he who denies it. The Atman is the basis of all kinds of knowledge. The Self is within, the Self is without, the Self is before and the Self is behind. The Self is on the right hand, the Self is on the left, the Self is above and the Self is below."

Brahman cannot be described, because description implies distinction. The objective world – the world of names and forms – has no independent existence. The Atman alone has real existence. The world is only *Vyavaharika* or phenomenal, *Maya* or illusion.

Shankara's teachings can be summed up in these words:

Brahma Satyam Jagat Mithya,
Jeevo Brahmaiva Na Aparah

Brahman alone is real, this world is unreal; the Jiva is identical with Brahman.

Shankara preached *Vivarta Vada.* Just as the snake is superimposed on the rope, this world and this body are superimposed on Brahman or the Supreme Self. If you acquire knowledge of the rope, the illusion of the snake will vanish. Likewise, if you receive knowledge of Brahman, the illusion of the body and the world will vanish.

Shankara may now have realised that his life was coming to an end. He therefore travelled to Kashmir to the temple of Mother Sharada, where no one from the south had ever been able to defeat the resident scholars and enter. Shankara managed this feat also and was allowed to enter the sanctum sanctorum.

After this, he is said to have gone to Nepal and thence to Kedarnath in the Himalayas, where he is supposed to have simply gone into a cave and disappeared in the biting cold.

The year was 820 AD and he was only 32. By defeating religious scholars from 72 different schools and establishing the superiority of Vedic thought, he proved he was the *Jagatguru.* True to the prophecy, he had a life as brilliant but short-lived as a meteorite.

❑ ❑ ❑

VARDHAMAN MAHAVIRA (599–527 BC)

The Great Conqueror

Vardhaman Mahavira was born in 599 BC to Siddhartha and Trishala. The family belonged to the Kshatriya or warrior caste. Siddhartha was the chief of Vaishali principality in Magadha (modern-day Bihar). Some accounts state his mother was a Brahmin, while others claim she was a Kshatriya. The young Vardhaman is supposed to have performed feats of great valour, earning the name, *Mahavira* (Great Hero).

During the 6th century BC, when Vardhaman was born, there was great societal unrest due to the overbearing attitude of the Brahmins towards the other supposedly lower castes. The Brahmins made increasingly stringent demands on the lower castes. For instance, the priestly caste demanded a large number of cattle as remuneration for performing the *Yagna* (fire sacrifice) and ancient Vedic rituals. Having to part with cattle placed an increasingly unbearable burden on the agricultural and trading castes. They began getting increasingly vociferous against the ritual of animal sacrifice perpetuated by the Brahmins.

It was in this atmosphere surcharged with revolt that Vardhaman lived, ultimately becoming one of the torchbearers of the revolt, preaching against ritualism and false beliefs perpetuated by the Brahmins. He also exhorted his followers that they must seek salvation through the path of penance and abstinence.

Although his formative years were spent in luxury, he did not have a materialistic bent of mind. In the year 569 BC, when he was 30, Mahavira renounced the world and began leading the life of an itinerant mendicant. This, despite the fact that he was married to Yashoda, and they already had a daughter called Priyadarshani. His renunciation came about after his parents passed away through the ritual of *sallekhana* or voluntary self-starvation, a tradition that is still occasionally practised by orthodox Jains.

Deeply influenced by this, like his parents, Mahavira joined the ascetic order of Parsvanatha, after distributing his wealth to the poor.

The Historical Founder

Although there is a popular misconception that Mahavira was the founder of Jainism, this is not the whole truth. He was, in fact, the 24th and last *Tirthankara* (prophet) of Jainism, which is said to be a 5,000-year-old ascetic tradition, making it one of the oldest religions in the world. Mahavira based most of his doctrines on the teachings of Parsvanatha, the 23rd *Tirthankara*, who was a 9th century BC teacher from Benares. It was Mahavira who ensured that all the earlier Jaina teachings and doctrines – including beliefs that were metaphysical, mythological and cosmological – were assimilated and codified into the Jaina religious order. Mahavira can therefore be considered the *historical* founder of Jainism, which was founded by the first *Tirthankara*, Rishabha.

For the next 12 years, he kept wandering from place to place. In the first year, he is said to have used only one garment to clothe himself. Later, he discarded even this, going about naked, not even retaining the traditional begging bowl that was also used for drinking water. Totally oblivious of his surroundings, he would meditate day and night at whatever place he happened to be in – a cremation, burial or open ground, at the foot of trees, wherever. Even if insects and other creatures crawled all over his body, he was impervious to their bites and stings. Needless to say, he presented an ungainly sight and invited a hostile reception at some places he visited.

As he wandered around, he would fast for long periods. When he ate, he ensured it was never anything that was specially prepared for him. In order to avoid injuring any form of life, he propounded his belief in *ahimsa* or non-violence. However, for four months during the monsoons, he would spend time in villages or towns.

After 12 years of severe austerities, Mahavira is said to have attained *kevala-jnana* (the highest knowledge or Enlightenment) in 557 BC, while seated under an Ashoka tree. Thereafter, he began preaching what he had practised for 12 years. Speaking against idol worship, Mahavira said that there was an immortal soul (*jiva*) within all living beings, which is why it was important to avoid hurting any living creature. The soul is, however, bound by the effects of karma, which causes it to suffer repeated rebirths. This suffering only ceases when the cycle of rebirth is broken after a person attains *moksha* or liberation, which was possible through penance, abstinence and asceticism.

The Five Truths

It was his belief in not hurting any creature that led the Jains to strictly practise vegetarianism. In due course of time, this led to the stoppage of animal sacrifice in ancient rituals. He revived the religious order (*Tirth*) of monks and nuns, known as the Jaina Sangha. Parsvanatha had taught people to live by four truths. Mahavira added another one and taught his disciples to live by the five truths: *Ahimsa* (non-violence); *Satya* (truth); *Asteya* (non-stealing); *Aparigraha* (non-possession) and *Brahmacharya* (chastity), the last one being added by Mahavira. He is said to have had 11 direct disciples or *Ganadhars*, who later compiled 12 Scriptures, *Agamas*, based on what Mahavira taught. These *Agamas* were passed orally from teacher to disciple for generations, before being finally put into writing 890 years after the death of Lord Mahavira.

While staying with King Hastipala of Pavapuri near Patna, Bihar, Mahavira breathed his last in 527 BC at the age of 72.

Mahavira is also called *Jina*, the Conqueror or the Victorious (over bondage, greed and attachment). The term 'Jain' is derived from this Sanskrit word, *Jina*. After differences on many issues, including idol worship, Mahavira's followers later split up into two sects, the *Digambars* (the sky-clad) and the *Svetambars* (the white-clad). While the former went about naked, the latter only used white garments. However, the fundamental views of both sects on ethics and philosophy are identical.

The primary goal of Jainism is for each individual to break the cycle of birth and death and become a perfected soul. Jainism does not believe in a Creator or God. What is said to exist is Pure Consciousness, which is a state of perfect knowledge, bliss, love and compassion. This state can be attained only when the multiple layers of karma are removed, allowing one to merge with Divine Consciousness.

Thanks to the enlightened teachings of Lord Mahavira, Jainism is today synonymous with love, compassion, asceticism, peace and non-violence, qualities as essential in the modern world as they were during Mahavira's time. Jainism is also the only religion that allows the spiritually enlightened person to hasten his or her own death through voluntary fasting. Today there are some six million Jains, most of them living in India.

GAUTAM BUDDHA (563–483 BC)

Prophet of the Middle Path

The founder of Buddhism and one of the greatest seers ever to have walked the earth, Gautam Buddha was born in 563 BC to Shuddodhana and Mayadevi in the village of Lumbini, near Kapilvastu, which now falls within the borders of Nepal. Many historical accounts claim his father was the King of Kapilvastu, although he was probably simply a very wealthy man and the head of the Sakya warrior clan. This is why Buddha was also known as *Sakyamuni* (Sage of the Sakyas).

Named Siddhartha, when he was just seven days old, his mother expired. Thereafter, his stepmother Gautami brought him up.

Legend has it that at his birth an astrologer had predicted the infant would renounce his throne and the world the day he saw misery, suffering and death. Concerned by this strange prediction, Shuddodhana decided to keep his son secluded from the outside world. Siddhartha had all the luxuries and worldly pleasures provided within the precincts of the palace.

In his young days itself, he was inclined toward introspection, which displeased his father, who wanted his son to be warrior, not a religious philosopher. When barely 16, he was married off to a beautiful princess, Yashodhara. Before long, they had a bonny boy whom they named Rahul. Their idyllic existence was soon to come to an end, however.

The Great Renunciation

One day, Siddhartha ventured out into the streets with only a servant for company. This was the first time he was stepping out thus. It was an outing that would change his life forever.

The young prince first saw a very old and feeble man, who could barely walk. Some way off, there was a man who was in a great deal of pain. Finally, he set eyes on a dead body for the first time. Having been insulated all his life from pain and suffering, he found these sights shocking. His servant explained matter-of-factly that pain, suffering and death were an inevitable part of life.

The young prince's psyche was scarred irrevocably, thanks to his father having kept him away from such sights all these years. Why was there so much misery in the world? What was the purpose of existence, he wondered, if death was inevitable? How could such acute human misery be avoided?

Siddhartha realised he would never find these answers in his palace. Renouncing his life of comfort and luxury, Siddhartha left his young son, Rahul, his wife and all other worldly possessions, determined to follow a life of privation and austerity in order to discover the root cause of suffering. There was no happiness in a life of materialistic pleasure when the rest of humanity was suffering, he decided. He had to find a path to *moksha* (salvation). The young man was all of 29 years old. Known as the Great Renunciation, this decision is celebrated as a historical turning point by Buddhists.

For the next six years, he lived the life of a wandering mendicant, trying to discover the root cause of suffering from all the sadhus and sages he came across. Subjecting his body to intense deprivation, he went without food for days together, meditating day and night, seeking an answer to his queries.

Investigating Hinduism, he sought answers from some renowned Brahmin teachers, without success. Furthermore, he found the caste system and sacrificial rituals abhorrent.

After a few fruitless years, during which time he seemed more a human skeleton, he realised the path of subjecting oneself to extreme hardship would get him nowhere. If he wanted to find salvation, he had to keep his body fit and strong. So he once again began taking food regularly.

Wandering from place to place, around 528 BC he reached Bodh Gaya in present-day Bihar. He was now 35. One evening, he sat beneath a giant banyan tree and kept meditating for hours. Prior to this, he had already succeeded in reaching higher states of consciousness. Suddenly, the Divine Light shone brightly and he felt a sudden gush of knowledge – he now had the answers to all his questions. He had at last attained *Nirvana* (Enlightenment) and found the way to salvation from suffering.

Thereafter, he would come to be known as the Buddha (the Enlightened One). It was in that profound state of Divine Consciousness that he realised it was futile searching for God without – the answers he had been seeking without had always been within!

Soon thereafter, he gave his first sermon in the Deer Park near Benares. This sermon contains the gist of Buddhism and its text is still preserved.

The Buddha's Teachings

For the next 45 years of his existence, the Buddha went about preaching that *desire was the root cause of all evil.* Clean-shaven and barefooted, he lived the life of a *bhikshu*, his only possessions being a saffron robe, a walking stick and the begging bowl. Man had to eliminate desire if he sought true peace and happiness. Empty rituals and rigorous austerity would lead one nowhere, he stressed. Rather than a life of either extreme, it was necessary to follow the middle path.

While preaching at Sarnath, he first spoke about the four noble truths and the Eightfold Path. The four noble truths were: sufferings exist in life; sufferings arise from attachment to desires; sufferings cease the moment attachment to desires cease; freedom from suffering is possible if one followed the Eightfold Path. Buddha exhorted the people to follow this Eightfold Path:

1. Right View
2. Right Thought
3. Right Speech
4. Right Conduct
5. Right Livelihood
6. Right Effort
7. Right Mindfulness
8. Right Concentration

All through his life, Buddha answered all questions of his disciples, except one – did God exist? Realising the futility of telling people that all that existed was Pure Consciousness, he preferred to hold his counsel on this count. Preaching against the caste system and other ills, he stressed that Righteous Living was more important than other narrow considerations.

With the country steeped in regressive practices that Hinduism had fallen into, many people were attracted to a religion that made no distinction between caste or creed and espoused the cause of compassion, non-violence and vegetarianism.

After attaining Nirvana, he returned for a brief period to his hometown and converted his father, wife and other family members to his beliefs. By the time he died in Kushinagar (Nepal) at the age of 80 in 483 BC, due to food poisoning, Buddhism had already begun attracting adherents across the country.

Before long, the religion spread to Burma, China, Sri Lanka, Japan and other south-east Asian countries. Nearly 2,500 years after his death, the Buddha's teachings are as relevant as when he first preached them.

❑ ❑ ❑

NAGARJUNA (150–250 AD)

The Reality of *Shunyata*

The greatest mystic from the Mahayana school of Buddhism, there are conflicting accounts about the precise details of his life. The earliest available biographical account of Nagarjuna is in Chinese, written around 405 AD by a renowned Buddhist translator, Kumarajiva (344–413 AD). Most accounts agree on the fact that Nagarjuna was born in a Brahmin family in South India, probably between 150 and 250 AD.

There is no historical data regarding his parents, childhood and early priestly training. However, his knowledge of several Hindu philosophical treatises supports the contention that he belonged to a Brahmin family of South India.

The legend goes that while still a boy, this young Brahmin had mastered the *Vedas* and all existing Hindu sciences, including black magic. He then entered a Buddhist monastery, seeking to enhance his knowledge. Thanks to his profound intellectual capability, he is said to have mastered the entire Pali canon, the early writings of Buddhism, within just 90 days. When he learned the profound meaning of the Mahayana

Buddhist doctrines, Nagarjuna underwent a spiritual transformation.

However, he was not totally satisfied with some of these tenets. Leaving the monastery, he went in search of more advanced teachings of the Buddha. The legend goes that one day he was teaching the Buddha's doctrine to a group of people. To his surprise, after his lecture he noticed that two members of the audience disappeared into the ground! He followed them underground to their home, the kingdom of the Nagas – half-divine, serpent-like beings. One of them turned out to be a *Mahanaga bodhisattva* (a chief serpent who was on the path to enlightenment). This individual presented him with the most profound verses of the Mahayana.

These writings were the *Prajnaparamitas*, the Perfection of Wisdom sutras. Centuries before, the Buddha had delivered these sacred teachings, but had later decided they were too profound for his contemporaries. These were therefore hidden in the nether world for safekeeping, until humankind had reached the right level of spiritual development that would ensure they could comprehend these teachings of "perfect wisdom". The time was now ripe to propagate these teachings and Nagarjuna was the chosen medium to preach Buddha's most profound teachings.

The Truth

As was his wont, Nagarjuna mastered these teachings in a short span of time. He then went around propagating these truths across the country, successfully defeating many opponents in philosophical debates, according to the prevailing custom. Nagarjuna's teachings led to the formation of the Madhyamika (Middle Path) School.

Based on Buddha's advocacy of the Middle Path that sought to avoid the two extremes of over-indulgence or overzealous austerity, Nagarjuna developed a rigorous dialectical logic through which every philosophical standpoint was reduced to a black hole of contradictions.

The Madhyamikas opined that neither existence nor non-existence could be asserted of the world and all else in it. Therefore, they refused to affirm or deny any philosophical proposition. Nagarjuna stressed that the mind must be liberated from its tendency to cling to cut-and-dried theories about the truth. The only truth was *Shunyata* – nothingness or void – and all other truths were inherently misleading. Relative truths were mere distortions of truth that could mislead seekers, unlike the pieces of a jigsaw puzzle that could add to the complete truth bit by bit.

Yet, these relative truths cannot be entirely repudiated, for the seeker could still learn to use them as aids, while bearing in mind that they are not accurate in themselves.

In his analytical verses, treatises, letters and hymns, Nagarjuna emphasised the practice of non-attachment – that is, perceiving the emptiness of all things and thereby being detached from them. Through logical arguments in the *Madhyamika Karika*, he criticised Buddhist as well as Hindu views on existence. His arguments were chiefly directed at the theories of existence put forward by the Buddhist schools of Sthaviravada and Sarvastivada. Nagarjuna held that the very nature of existence is relational; all things are devoid of absolute reality and exist only in relation to a context, a condition. Whatever can be conceptualised is relative, and whatever is relative is *shunya* or empty.

Nagarjuna's stress on *Shunyata* should not be mistaken for negativity. In fact, *Shunyata* implies the unchanging, deathless, unqualified Reality.

Critical Works

Within a hundred years of Nagarjuna's death, many disciples honoured him as a Buddha. By the 3rd century onward, Buddhist traditions in India, China, Tibet, Japan and Korea were greatly influenced by Nagarjuna's thoughts. Although many treatises have been credited to this great Buddhist philosopher, it seems likely that other Buddhist teachers may have probably written some of these.

Two Sanskrit treatises, however, are considered written by Nagarjuna himself: *Mula Madhyamika Karikas* (*Fundamentals of the Middle Way*) and *Vigrahayyavartani* (*Treatise on Averting the Arguments*). Both the works clearly represent his beliefs, critically analysing false views about the nature of existence, the means of knowledge and the nature of Reality.

There are other important Madhyamika texts in Chinese and Tibetan that are attributed to Nagarjuna. Tibetan tradition also credits a large number of tantric and medical treatises to Nagarjuna. Whether these were actually the works of Nagarjuna is largely unsubstantiated. The confusion on authorship primarily arose because there were other sages and philosophers who went by the same name.

Two schools of thought on Nagarjuna's works arose by the 5th century, the Bhavaviveka and the Buddhapalita. While the former held that the Madhyamika philosophy was positive in thought, the latter held that every viewpoint, including their own, could be reduced to absurdity, and this fact alone could lead to *prajna* (intuitive insight) and Enlightenment. It is the Buddhapalita school of thought that deeply influenced Tibetan Buddhist traditions as well as those that ultimately culminated in Japan's Zen Buddhism.

Like his early years, nothing much is known about the philosopher's last days. Although some accounts claim Nagarjuna visited China, there is no evidence to back this up. It was purely Kumarajiva's arrival in China after the Han Dynasty that played an instrumental role in the spread of Nagarjuna's teachings in China.

❑ ❑ ❑

SWAMI DAYANAND SARASWATI (1824–1883)

The Iconoclastic Seer

If ever there was an iconoclastic guru who walked this land of sages, it had to be Swami Dayanand Saraswati.

Born in 1824 to a wealthy Brahmin, Karshanji Lalji Tiwari, at a small town called Tankara in the state of Morvi, Saurashtra, he was christened Moolashankar Tiwari. Moolashankar's mother, Amrithbai, was a religious woman. Karshanji too believed in faithfully following all the traditional religious practices.

The boy's education began when he was five and he was made to learn all the religious practices. By the time he was 14, he knew the *Yajurveda*, the *Upanishads* and other Scriptures by heart. It was Karshanji's desire that his son should also become a devotee of Shiva, like he was. Moolashankar, though, did not like his father's overbearing attitude.

The young boy looked up to his uncle, who was a simple, religious and learned man. It was his uncle who had a deep influence on Moolashankar.

Eye-opening Night

An incident that occurred one Shivarathri night changed Moolashankar's life irrevocably. As was the custom, all devotees of Lord Shiva had gathered at the local temple, ready to stay awake all through the night to worship Shiva. Well past midnight, however, all the devotees fell off to sleep one after another. Except the young Moolashankar, who was determined to stay awake and sat gazing at the Shivalinga.

Suddenly, a few mice appeared from the dark corners, climbed upon the Shivalinga, romped about and began nibbling at the offerings. The boy was amazed. His father had always told him that Lord Shiva was all-powerful. Then how could these puny mice dance all over the Shivalinga without any response from the linga to this affront? He woke his father and questioned him about this. The irritated Karshanji had no response to his son's logical reasoning. The young boy had learnt his first iconoclastic lesson – the futility of idol worship.

When Moolashankar was 14, cholera broke out in Morvi and his sister succumbed to the disease. This tragedy aroused deep questions about death in the youngster. Three years later, it was his beloved uncle who fell victim to the disease. Moolashankar was shaken to the core by this death. His aversion to all worldly things took firm root. Realising the futility of man's shallow existence, the young man had profound queries that sought coherent answers. Concluding that only a genuine guru could answer him, he was determined to turn his back on materialistic existence.

The growing sense of alienation and detachment was not lost on his parents, who wasted no time in looking out for a suitable match for him. When preparations for his marriage were underway, Moolashankar decided the time was ripe to run away from home in search of a suitable guru.

One evening, as the dark shadows around his house were lengthening, Moolashankar walked out, determined never to return home. Although his father later tried everything to get his son back home, it was all in vain.

The Search Ends

All of 21 years, Moolashankar went to Baroda, Ahmedabad, Hardwar, Kashi, Kanpur and other places in his budding quest for a guru. Day and night, across mountains and forests, he walked hundreds of miles. Finally, he heard of a swami who lived in Mathura. This was perhaps the guru he was seeking.

On November 14, 1860, he reached the doorsteps of Swami Virajananda Saraswati, 15 years after he had begun his quest. When 36-year-old Moolashankar knocked on the door, saying he had come to seek spiritual enlightenment, Virajananda enquired whether he knew grammar. When Moolashankar mentioned the two Sanskrit texts he had mastered, he was asked to throw "those useless books" into the river Yamuna as a precondition for admittance.

Without a moment's hesitation, Moolashankar complied. The doors of the ashram were now open to him. On entering, he was amazed. Swami Virajananda was blind!

Moolashankar was later rechristened Swami Dayanand Saraswati. Over the next few years, this blind guru would teach him that the pantheon of Hindu gods was a myth and there was only one god, one reality – Brahman. The only Scripture was the *Vedas*, which had everything there was to know. If you knew the *Vedanta* – *Ved* means 'knowledge' and *anta* signifies the end of knowledge – you knew everything there was to know in the cosmos.

His education over, Dayanand promised to preach the *Vedas* to the people and took leave of his guru. Travelling across the country, he visited towns and cities preaching the *Vedas* and decrying idol worship: "Idol worship is not mentioned in the *Vedas*. The rational mind cannot accept idol worship. God is everywhere. God has no shape or form."

For orthodox Hindus and the pundits, this was nothing but heresy. Yet, in debate after debate on the Scriptures, he was able to rout even the most learned of Brahmins. True to his form, he shred the hypocrisy in all religions, be it Hinduism,

Christianity or any other. He exhorted the people to follow the religion outlined in the *Vedas*.

While the British were initially pleased when he attacked Hindu religious practices, they squirmed in discomfort when he turned his critical gaze on Christianity. A nationalist to the core, he is also said to have participated in the 1857 War of Independence. Before long, as he kept gathering adherents across the country, the list of his sworn enemies kept increasing. Perturbed at his "rantings", they decided that this swami was better dead than alive.

Assassination Attempts

Then began the attempts to murder him, especially through poison. However, Dayanand was strong as a bull, thanks to his regular practice of Hatha Yoga and Pranayam. Although he was poisoned on quite a few occasions, each time he is said to have thrown up the poison through his yogic prowess.

On October 22, 1869, he reached Benares (Kashi), where he had been invited by all the scholars to take part in a great debate. Over 50,000 people are said to have attended this debate. Pitted against Dayanand were 27 distinguished scholars and dozens of other learned pundits of Kashi. In round after round, Dayanand defeated these great scholars.

To get the better of him, a trick was then played. A scholar handed Dayanand two sheets of paper with a longwinded, nonsensical question. As Dayanand spent a few minutes trying to comprehend it, the Maharaja of Kashi – who was playing the interlocutor – declared that Dayanand had been "defeated", since he was unable to answer the question.

But the Press played spoilsport by publishing the actual turn of events, giving a further boost to Dayanand's already towering reputation. He became a national hero!

In 1873, Dayanand met Keshab Chandra Sen in Calcutta, who gently told him that if he preached in the common man's language, rather than in Sanskrit, his ideas would get across faster. Thereafter, Swamiji ensured that he spoke in Hindi and wrote all his books in Hindi, too.

Realising that his ideas and ideals might not outlive his mortal body, on April 10, 1875 he established the Arya Samaj (Noble Society). To propagate his ideals, he wrote a book, *Satyartha Prakash* (Light of Truth). Not one to pull his punches, Dayanand condemned the caste system, child marriage, untouchability, purdah and other social evils. He was all in favour of widow remarriage, about which he spoke forcefully even at the 1876 Kumbh Mela in Hardwar. He insisted that women should have equal rights with men.

His brusque and forthright manner led to his ultimate elimination. He is said to have severely criticised the Jodhpur Raja's concubine. The enraged woman then bribed the palace cook to poison his food. Having heard of his legendary yogic prowess, she also ensured that ground glass was mixed with the food. Although Dayanand vomited the poison through his yogic powers, the ground glass entered his bloodstream, proving fatal.

Amazingly, he survived for a few agony-filled weeks. Overcome by remorse, the cook confessed. True to his calling, the swami who never suffered fools gave the cook some money so that the man could flee before his followers heard of the cook's role in the poisoning and lynched him.

Having fought to the very last breath, Swami Dayanand Saraswati (whom Vivekananda called "great") breathed his last on October 30, 1883.

❑ ❑ ❑

SRI RAMAKRISHNA PARAMAHANSA (1836–1886)

The Supreme Seer

One of the greatest souls in the annals of Indian spiritual history, Ramakrishna was born Gadadhar (the macebearer) Chattopadhyaya in a poor Brahmin family on February 18, 1836 at the little village of Kamarpukur, near Calcutta in Bengal.

From his very early years, Ramakrishna had an intensely spiritual streak, which is not surprising considering that both his parents were very pious individuals. Occasionally, Ramakrishna would go into a spiritual trance and temporarily lose consciousness.

On the first occasion, when he was barely six, he went into a state of rapture while watching some cranes in flight moving across a storm cloud. And on another occasion, he was lost to the outer world while playing Lord Shiva in a school play.

Temple Priest

Thanks to the family's impoverished background, although a Brahmin, he was barely educated. In 1852, his brother Ramkumar called him to Calcutta, where he was serving as a temple priest at the Dakshineshwar Kali temple, established by a lady called Rani Rashmoni. Although not the most popular calling even in those days, this was one occupation that allowed Ramakrishna to indulge in what he loved most – immersing himself in intense meditation and other spiritual rituals that would take him closer to God and God-realisation.

Ramkumar died in 1856 and this meant that Ramakrishna was now the sole priest of the temple of Goddess Kali, located on the banks of the Ganges near Calcutta.

His constant absorption in spiritual thoughts ensured he had frequent spiritual and mystic experiences, where he would merge with the Absolute Reality. Ramakrishna was a guru who was not constrained by thoughts of one discipline or approach being the "right" one. He believed in the universalism of all religions. From idol worship to Advaita, Vaishnava, Yoga, Tantra and all other forms or practices of Hinduism, he tried them all to reach Divine Consciousness. Not content with this, he turned to Christianity and Islam. Much to his pleasant surprise, he found that all paths led him to the same experience of Divine Bliss or Ultimate Reality.

Which is why the seer said: "Different people call [God] by different names: some as Allah, some as God, and others as Krishna, Shiva and Brahman. It is like the water in a lake. Some drink it at one place and call it 'jal', others at another place and call it 'pani', and still others at a third place and call it 'water'. The Hindus call it 'jal', the Christians 'water', and the Moslems 'pani'. But it is one and the same thing."

Divine Experience

Having thus had first-hand experience of the Divine Truth, he proclaimed that all religious of the world were essentially one, as all the different paths led to the same goal: "As many faiths, so many paths."

He did not decry idol worship, but felt it was a legitimate way of seeking the Divine. He revealed that it was through his intense devotion to the image of the Divine Mother in Dakshineshwar that Realisation had come to him. Meditating in a sacred grove of trees near the temple grounds, he sought another vision of the Goddess Kali. When this did not happen for quite some time, he became frustrated and threatened to kill himself with a ritual dagger normally held in the hands of the Goddess.

Suddenly, he had a Divine experience: *"When I jumped up like a madman and seized* [a sword], *suddenly the blessed Mother revealed herself. The buildings with their different parts, the temple, and everything vanished from my sight, leaving no trace whatsoever, and in their stead I saw a limitless, infinite, effulgent Ocean of Consciousness. As far as the eye could see, the shining billows were madly rushing at me from all sides with a terrific noise, to swallow me up. I was caught in the rush and collapsed, unconscious... within me there was a steady flow of undiluted bliss, altogether new, and I felt the presence of the Divine Mother."*

Eccentric Behaviour

As time passed, Ramakrishna's behaviour seemed more and more eccentric, becoming a cause of concern to his near and dear ones. On and off, he would identify himself with religious and mythical figures. Hoping to curb this "mental instability", his parents decided to get him married as it was felt that celibacy could be causing him problems. At the age of 19, he was married to Sharada Devi.

Ma Sharada Devi

However, a holy woman called Bhairavi Brahmani – who later became his first guru – concluded that Ramakrishna's was a "spiritual madness" and nothing else. People thereafter treated him with more respect.

Years later, when the child-bride Sharada had matured, she went to meet her "eccentric" husband. Somehow, she recognised the great soul in him. Instead of being her husband, he became her guru. Throughout their married life, the relationship was totally devoid of any sexual element. In the days to come, Sharada would herself be recognised as a realised soul.

Ramakrishna now adopted the life of a renunciate. Through his second guru Totapuri (a wandering ascetic from the Naga sect), he also learnt about the non-dualist philosophy of Advaita Vedanta, which considers God to be a formless Unmanifest Energy that permeates the cosmos. During this period, Ramakrishna experienced a deep form of trance referred to as *Nirvikalpa Samadhi* – a state of complete absorption of the soul into the Divine Ocean of Consciousness.

It was this multiplicity of experiences that facilitated his understanding of all forms of worship. Which is why, at different times, the seer explained to his followers that God was both formed and formless and would appear to a devotee in whichever way the latter believed in. Therefore, he taught each devotee about God according to the devotee's line of thinking. He exhorted his devotees: "Remain always strong and steadfast in your own faith, but eschew all bigotry and intolerance."

Seeking to reaffirm the ancient truths of Hinduism, Ramakrishna trained a devoted band of followers. The man he appointed as his torchbearer was no less a persona than he was – his disciple Narendranath, popularly called Swami Vivekananda. Although Ramakrishna's teachings were nothing new, under the onslaught of the Christian missionaries and British colonists, Indians had to be reminded of their rich Vedic heritage. As Vivekananda put it, Ramakrishna brought old truths to light.

Truth through Parables

Like Jesus Christ and other great religious teachers, he often spoke in parables. Questioned about the existence of evil, Ramakrishna had this to say: "Evil exists in God as poison in a serpent. What is poison to us is not poison to the serpent. Evil is evil only from the point of view of man." In other words, from the absolute viewpoint, there is no such thing as "evil". "Evil" exists as a terrible reality only from a relative human perspective.

It was such an intense form of Realisation that held him aloft from all forms of sex-consciousness. This was why he could approach men and women with the innocence and simplicity of a child. Declaring that human beings were the highest manifestations of God, he had an intense love for humanity. His teachings inspired the formation of the Ramakrishna Mission – the first monastic order in India devoted to serving humanity.

His philosophy influenced many famous writers and philosophers, including Aldous Huxley, Arnold Toynbee, Leo Tolstoy, Christopher Isherwood and Mahatma Gandhi.

On August 16, 1886 Ramakrishna succumbed to cancer of the throat. By this time, he was already well known as 'Paramahansa' – the Supreme Swan.

❑ ❑ ❑

SWAMI VIVEKANANDA (1863–1902)

The Agnostic-turned-Seer

When Narendranath Dutta was born on January 12, 1863 in Calcutta, few would have imagined that he would one day be counted amongst India's greatest seers. The son of Vishwanath and Bhuvaneshwari Dutta, as a child Narendra was always bubbling with mischief.

A lawyer by profession, Vishwanath Dutta would always advise his son that he need not fear "so long as you keep to the path of truth and dharma". Narendra's inquisitiveness and sense of inquiry was evident from his formative years. So was his compassion for others. If a beggar asked for alms, the young lad would give away anything he had, much to the displeasure of his mother.

During his childhood, whenever his mother told him tales from the *Ramayana*, he would listen fascinated. One day, his mother even caught him pretending he was Lord Shiva. Would he also become a sannyasi like his grandfather, his mother wondered. Yet, there were other interests too. His affluent background afforded him the opportunity to learn music and singing.

In 1880, Narendra cleared his Matriculation, securing the First Division, and joined college. His voracious appetite for knowledge only kept increasing by the day and he would devour books from the library that were not even in the curriculum. Well read in history, science and Western philosophy, he yearned to learn about the secrets of Creation and God.

Doubts and Scepticism

But the more he read, the more his doubts and uncertainties grew. He spoke to many a learned soul, seeking answers. However, none of them had any convincing answers to his searching queries. It was at this juncture that he was attracted to the atheistic teachings of Herbert Spencer and developed a deeply sceptical streak.

Around this time, the air was abuzz with talk of a priest at the temple of Goddess Ḳali in Dakshineshwar, who was said to have realised God. Curious, Narendra went to meet him along with his friends.

The man was Ramakrishna Paramahansa, who would, in the days to come, change the thinking of the sceptical Narendra and show him the path to God. Narendra asked Ramakrishna whether he had seen God.

Not only had he seen God, but he could also show God to the young man, if his desire was so strong, the seer responded. Narendra continued to be sceptical, convinced that the illiterate priest was deranged!

However, he kept going back to meet Ramakrishna, not wanting to jump to conclusions without having investigated the matter himself. In their meetings, it became clear that Narendra rejected idol worship, mystic experiences and the theory of Advaita (monism). There were many paths to reach God, the unperturbed Ramakrishna reasoned with Narendra: "It is improper to pass judgement on anything that one does not understand."

Wishing to test the young man, Ramakrishna once told him: "I have attained some powers after a long period of meditation. They will give whatever a man wants. I have given up all desire, and so I have no use for these powers. Shall I bestow these powers on you?"

Narendra inquired whether these would help him realise God. No, said the seer. Then, said Narendra, he was not interested in these powers. All he was interested in was to realise God. His reply convinced Ramakrishna that Narendra was now ready to realise the Self.

Gradually, Ramakrishna began grooming Narendra and passing on his powers to the youngster.

When Narendra's parents got wind of this, their response was typically Indian – get him married! But by then Narendra had already trod onto the path of renunciation.

When Narendra passed his BA examination in 1884, tragedy struck the family. Vishwanath Dutta passed away. With the family breadwinner no more, poverty struck the family like a thunderbolt. Creditors were now breathing down their neck and the once-prosperous family was reduced to near starvation, with Narendra fainting on the streets from sheer hunger as he went around desperately looking for a job. He then began working as a teacher at Vidyasagar School.

Handling the Baton

Some time later, his guru developed throat cancer. Narendra threw up his job in order to nurse Ramakrishna. Before long, the guru was no more, but not before he had passed the baton to Narendra. A monastery was established at Baranagar, with Narendra and 11 other inmates committed to spreading the Master's word, the service of humankind and their own Realisation.

Narendra began travelling all over the country, preaching the essence of the *Vedas* and Hinduism, trying to arouse Indians from their slumber. He travelled long distances on foot, only taking trains when somebody was kind enough to purchase his ticket. He exhorted all the upper castes to work for the uplift of the downtrodden. He preached that the salvation of mankind was more important than personal salvation.

Having travelled the north, Narendra then went south. After being in Rameswaram for some time, he ended his countrywide trip at Kanyakumari. At the southern tip of India, he swam out to an outcrop of rocks in the sea and sat on it, meditating upon India's sorry state of affairs and all that he had witnessed in the past few years. Casteism had to be rooted out if India wished to rise to her former glory, he concluded. The world would also have to be made aware of the rich spiritual heritage that existed in India.

It was on this rock that the flame called Narendranath Dutta was fully transformed into the luminous seer called Swami Vivekananda.

During his sojourn across India, Vivekananda heard about the Parliament of Religions that was to be held in Chicago.

With contributions pouring in from all over the country, he sailed for America on May 31, 1893. When he finally reached Chicago, he was three months before schedule. Unsure of the date of opening, of how to register himself and about who would recommend his name as a delegate and speaker, he nevertheless knew that God would finally take care of everything.

The Mesmerising Speech

The Parliament opened on September 11, 1893. He had already managed to get his name on the list of delegates and speakers. However, when it was his turn to speak, sheer nervousness made him pass up his turn more than once. Finally, he requested the president of the Parliament to let him speak last.

When his moment of reckoning came, he spoke without any prepared text. "Sisters and brothers of America..." as his pleasant voice rang across the hall, the audience broke into spontaneous applause that echoed uninterrupted for three minutes. His speech was short but sweet: people of different religions finally reach the same God, just as a river born in different places finally reaches the same sea. In essence, he stressed, no religion was superior, none inferior. Appealing for universal tolerance, he said that what counted was man's faith, not which faith he belonged to.

The entire American nation was agog after hearing this saffron-robed swami from India. After travelling and speaking across America, he reached England, where he impressed all who heard and met him. One of those to come under his spell and who later came to India to devote her life for the common good was Margaret Noble, later famous as Sister Nivedita.

On February 20, 1897 he finally reached Calcutta. Everywhere, he was accorded a hero's welcome, with enormous crowds thronging the streets. In this year itself, he began the Ramakrishna Mission to further the ideals of his guru, Sri Ramakrishna. Within a couple of years, buildings were constructed on a plot of land at Belur on the banks of the Ganges, where the Ramakrishna Matha was established.

Four Classics

In June 1899, he sailed across to the West on his second visit. Over the next three years, he kept travelling, speaking, writing, preaching the *Vedanta* and the *Upanishads* and generally trying to arouse the nation from its centuries-long slumber.

He tried to make every Indian feel proud and declared: "The background, the Reality, of everyone is that same Eternal, Ever Blessed, Ever Pure, and Ever Perfect One. It is the Atman, the Soul, in the saint and the sinner, in the happy and the miserable, in the beautiful and the ugly, in men and in animals; it is the same throughout. It is the Shining One."

Besides numerous poems and other forms of writing, he left four classics: *Jnana-Yoga*, *Bhakti-Yoga*, *Karma-Yoga*, and *Raja-Yoga*, all outstanding treatises on Hindu philosophy.

Despite his boundless energy, the swami's non-stop activities were slowly beginning to tell on his health. On July 4, 1902 Swami Vivekananda breathed his last.

For further information, contact:

Ramakrishna Mission Institute of Culture

Gol Park

Kolkata - 700 029

INDIA

Tel: (33) 2464-1303, 2466-1235

Fax: (33) 2464-1307

E-mail: *rmic@vsnl.com*

❑ ❑ ❑

SRI AUROBINDO GHOSE (1872–1950)

The Superconscious Seer

When Ackroyd Ghose – Sri Aurobindo's childhood name – was born at Calcutta on August 15, 1872, his English-oriented father was determined to make his Indian son more English than the Englishmen. Beginning with christening his son with an English name, he later sent him off to Cambridge, England for schooling, when he was just seven years old. Until then, Aurobindo was being educated at Darjeeling.

For the next 14 years, Ackroyd lived abroad, learning English, Latin, Greek and French… anything except Indian languages, as his England-educated physician father wished to ensure his son was not corrupted by any pernicious Indian influence. Ironically, Ackroyd's father also passed instructions that he was to learn "nothing about any religion whatsoever".

His foreign schooling completed, Ackroyd was returning to India in 1893, when the news spread that the ship he was travelling in had sunk. Ackroyd's father died of shock on hearing this. For the young man, this turned out to be a blessing in disguise. He was now freed from the clutches of a father who had a warped Anglo-oriented mind.

Although Ackroyd cleared the Indian Civil Service exam, his first anti-English leaning surfaced when he refused to appear for the horse-riding test, which was mandatory. Reluctant to serve the British, he worked with Sister Nivedita for some time. During this period, he did something that would have made his father wince in horror had he been alive - he reinvented and Indiannised himself.

Born-again Indian

Rechristening himself Aurobindo, he began learning Indian languages and traditions with characteristic gusto. He began with Bengali, his mother tongue, and then learnt Hindi, Marathi, Gujarati and Sanskrit. Learning Sanskrit meant that a treasure trove of ancient Indian wisdom was thereafter open to him.

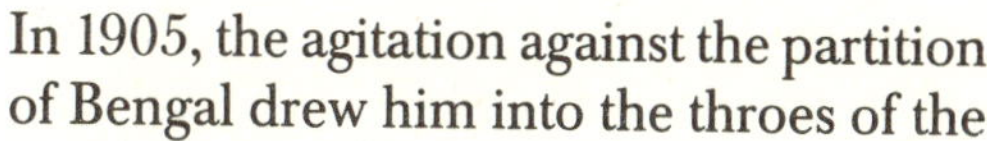

In 1905, the agitation against the partition of Bengal drew him into the throes of the nationalist and political movement. He is said to have led a secret organisation that sought to overthrow the British yoke. He began two newspapers, *Bande Mataram* and *Jugantar*, which wrote editorial after editorial decrying the oppressive British Raj. With their regular fulminations against the Raj, the boycott of foreign goods, the importance of social unity, the need of national schools to imbue traditional values in education and other such "seditious" thoughts, these papers stoked nationalistic fervour.

Seeking to throttle these "subversive" actions, the British imprisoned him in Alipur jail, where he would spend a year. This was to change his life. Aurobindo spent most of his time in practising Yoga and reading the Indian Scriptures.

In jail, his spiritual advancement was rapid. He is said to have had a series of mystic experiences. As he climbed one spiritual peak after another, he was later to claim that the spirit of Swami Vivekananda guided him along the path. This was probably the time when he gained Enlightenment and went into a totally spiritual orbit. He realised that it was a grave mistake to combat the British with their own means. Instead, India had to utilise what she was best at – her spiritual prowess.

Although a case of sedition was filed against him in 1907, his political career had already begun playing out its end game. He no longer believed in violent nationalism and came out with a book, *On Nationalism.* This was a collection of editorials enunciating his belief that social action without spiritual sustenance was futile.

Freed from prison, he withdrew from political life and announced he was retiring to Pondicherry. This was a masterstroke as Pondicherry was not under British rule, being a French dominion. Here, he set up an ashram and plunged into spiritual pursuits and, by and by, learnt the four major South Indian languages. The measure of Aurobindo's rising standing can be gauged from the fact that no less a stalwart than Mohandas Karamchand Gandhi was influenced by Aurobindo's thoughts and adopted his ideals.

Mahatma Gandhi later went to the extent of offering Aurobindo the reigns of the Congress Party, if he agreed to come out of seclusion. Aurobindo spurned this offer, much to the chagrin of nationalists. But Aurobindo's thinking was forthright. Of what use was political freedom when spiritual shackles were still in place? Political freedom would come inevitably, Aurobindo believed. What counted were efforts for spiritual emancipation. And this was Aurobindo's ultimate goal – the spiritual ascent of humankind – rather than just the political emancipation of India.

The Ascent to Superman

At the Pondicherry Ashram, Aurobindo's mystic visions continued, for he came up with a spate of books that throbbed with spiritual wisdom of the highest order. This was the true wisdom of a seer, not something culled from pedantic sources. In a short span of four years, Aurobindo came up with book after book overflowing with cosmic wisdom.

Although Aurobindo preached a philosophy that was rooted in Vedantic thought, interspersed with yogic practices and elements of Tantra, he added a new dimension to it. Mankind, said the modern seer, was on an evolutionary ascent that would ultimately see the rise of a Superman with Super-consciousness. He termed this Integral Yoga (*Purna Yoga*).

Essentially, this theory is aligned with the hundredth-monkey phenomenon. Over millennia, mankind has seen a higher and higher number of people gain Enlightenment or Cosmic Consciousness. Beyond a critical number, there would come a time when almost the entire human race attains Cosmic Consciousness. This was the goal he sought to promote. The seer, however, rejected any ideas of renunciation or the negation of the physical plane, unlike many ancient and some modern philosophers.

His essays on the *Bhagavad Gita* and commentaries on the *Upanishads* were erudition of the highest order. The Vedas, he insisted, were not hymns composed by migrating people meant to worship Nature – a contention then popular in the West, which he debunked. The Vedas, the seer declared in his book *The Secret of the Vedas*, were sacred Scriptures of Hinduism. The 68 published volumes he wrote in those four prolific years included *Essays on the Gita* (1921–28), *The Life Divine* (1940), *The Synthesis of Yoga* (1948), *The Human Cycle*, *The Life Divine*, *The Ideal of Human Unity* (all three published in 1949), *Savitri* (1950), and *On the Veda* (1956).

On November 26, 1926, Sri Aurobindo – as he now came to be called – retired into seclusion, a period that is generally regarded as the official establishment of his spiritual community. Confining himself to his rooms, he went on month-long fasts, no longer made a public appearance, rarely spoke and communicated mostly by writing. To immerse himself in meditation and yogic practices, he could now afford the luxury of seclusion as he had handed over active running of the Ashram to his spiritual partner, Mira Richard (1878–1973), popularly called the Mother. It was galling for many Indian disciples that a Frenchwoman of Egyptian origin, who had joined the Ashram in 1914, should oversee its running, but Aurobindo was no longer prey to such insular thinking.

The Mother

One of India's greatest seers and mystics, Sri Aurobindo passed away on December 5, 1950. By then, the Ashram had begun attracting people from all over the globe, with no less a person than Aldous Huxley having paid Aurobindo a visit.

After his death, the Mother continued advancing his dream. In 1968, work began to construct a utopian city, Auroville, which now functions according to Aurobindo's precepts and seeks to develop the New Man.

For further information, contact:

Sri Aurobindo Ashram

Pondicherry – 605 002

INDIA

Tel: (0413) 2262-2239

E-mail: *bureaucentral@mailroom.com*

❑ ❑ ❑

DR SARVEPALLI RADHAKRISHNAN (1888–1975)

The Great Teacher

One of modern India's great philosophers and teachers, Dr Sarvepalli Radhakrishnan was born on September 5, 1888 at Tiruttani, 40 miles north-east of Madras, in what is now Andhra Pradesh. The second son of a poor Brahmin couple, there was nothing about the young Radhakrishnan that hinted he was destined to be one of India's greatest scholars and statesmen. His life during those formative years is said to have been an ongoing struggle against adverse circumstances. He spent his early years at his hometown Tiruttani and at Tirupati, both pilgrim centres. During these years, he is said to have been influenced by reading the letters of Swami Vivekananda and Veer Savarkar's account of India's First War of Independence in 1857.

While graduating from Madras University with a Master's degree, he wrote a thesis on the *Vedanta* that was titled, *The Ethics of the Vedanta and its Metaphysical Presuppositions.* This thesis was prompted by the ludicrous charge that the *Vedanta* lacked ethics! In his thesis, he commented: "Religious feeling must establish itself as a rational way of living. If ever the spirit is to be at home in this world, and not merely a prisoner or a fugitive, spiritual foundations must be laid deep and preserved worthily. Religion must express itself in reasonable thought, fruitful action and right social institutions."

Radhakrishnan had a spiritual bent of mind that comes through clearly in all his writings. Perhaps this was one of the reasons why he did not participate in India's struggle for independence, which, despite Mahatma Gandhi's best efforts, kept lapsing into spirals of violence time and again.

Having secured his Master of Arts degree, he took to teaching as a profession. He was first appointed as a teacher at the Department of Philosophy in Madras Presidency College in April 1909. Thereafter, the study of Indian philosophy and religion was a serious preoccupation with Radhakrishnan.

His next major posting was in 1918 as Professor of Philosophy at the University of Mysore. Then, in 1921, came his appointment in the philosophy chair at the University of Calcutta. In September 1926, he represented the University of Calcutta at the International Congress of Philosophy in Harvard University. In his address to the Philosophical Congress, he stressed on the lack of spiritual growth in modern civilisation. He had now come to the notice of the West and was offered the post of Principal, Manchester College, Oxford, in 1929. It was an offer that he didn't take up, though.

His sojourns abroad during this period gave him the opportunity to deliver lectures to British students on Comparative Religion, which delighted him. As he put it, "It was a great experience for me to preach from Christian pulpits in Oxford and Birmingham, in Manchester and Liverpool. It heartened me to know that my addresses were liked by Christian audiences." For an Indian in those days, this was indeed no mean achievement.

He was Vice-Chancellor of Andhra University between 1931 and 1936. From 1936 to 1939, Dr Radhakrishnan was the Spalding Professor of Eastern Religions and Ethics at Oxford University. And he was elected Fellow of the British Academy in 1939.

Statesman and President

Three years later, he was back in India, serving as the Vice-Chancellor of the Benares Hindu University from 1939 to 1948. Around the time of Independence, he took up assignments that saw his entry into politics. But given his spiritual leanings, he was less of a politician and more of a statesman. He acted as the leader of the Indian delegation to UNESCO during 1946–52. He was also Indian Ambassador to the USSR between 1949 and 1952.

From 1952–62, he served as India's Vice-President, during which time he was also Chancellor of the University of Delhi (1953–62). He was elected to the office of the President of India in May 1962, when then President Dr Rajendra Prasad passed away, and was President up to May 1967. Thereafter, he retired from politics.

This philosopher-statesman was also an excellent writer. Thanks to his excellent command over English, he wrote many books that popularised India's ancient traditions in the West. He wrote on all religions of the world and his works include *Indian Philosophy* (1923), *The Philosophy of the Upanishads* (1924), *The Hindu View of Life* (1932), *Eastern Religions and Western Thought* (1939), *East and West: Some Reflections* (1955).

In numerous lectures too, he interpreted the Indian Scriptures for the benefit of Western audiences. He spoke in favour of a modern form of Hinduism that would embrace all world religions. He believed that India's progress lay in promoting a casteless and classless society.

Dr Sarvepalli Radhakrishnan passed away on April 17, 1975. In recognition of this great teacher, his birth date, September 5, is celebrated as Teacher's Day in India.

JIDDU KRISHNAMURTI (1895–1986)

The Pathless Guru

One of the few seers ever who did not quote other masters or the holy books, Jiddu Krishnamurti was born on May 11, 1895 in the village of Madanapalle, South India, to a pious middle-class family.

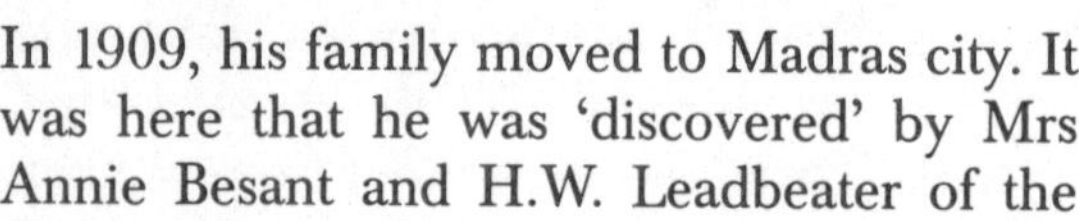

In 1909, his family moved to Madras city. It was here that he was 'discovered' by Mrs Annie Besant and H.W. Leadbeater of the Theosophical Society. The President of the Theosophical Society, Mrs Besant adopted him and proclaimed that he was the New Messiah the Theosophists had been waiting for. Three years later, she took him to England to have him educated for his future role as the World Teacher. In 1911, an organisation was formed for this specific purpose, The Order of the Star of the East.

The script of the Theosophists went awry when Krishnamurti had "certain mystical experiences" that deeply transformed his outlook. After his Illumination, he immediately realised the futility of the role he was being groomed to play. Following years of introspection and self-questioning, he made a firm resolve.

On August 3, 1929, Jiddu Krishnamurti dropped a bombshell on the opening day of the annual Star Camp at Ommen, Holland. In clear and unequivocal terms, he told his followers that he was forthwith disbanding the organisation founded by his foster mother.

As his stunned audience listened in silence, he said: "I maintain that truth is a pathless land, and you cannot approach it by any path whatsoever, by any religion, by any sect. That is my point of view, and I adhere to that absolutely and unconditionally. Truth, being limitless, unconditioned, unapproachable by any path whatsoever, cannot be organised; nor should any organisation be formed to lead or to coerce people along any particular path. If you first understand that, then you will see how impossible it is to organise a belief. A belief is purely an individual matter, and you cannot and must not organise it. If you do, it becomes dead, crystallised; it becomes a creed, a sect, a religion, to be imposed on others."

Pure Insight

From 1929 onward, Krishnamurti dissociated himself from all organised ideologies and religions. Until he breathed his last in 1986, he walked alone, simply meeting, talking and discussing with people from all parts of the world, not as a guru, but purely as a friend. For 65 years, he remained a globetrotter, distilling his wisdom to people in India, Europe, Australia and North and South America. His talks flowed from his profound insight into the most complex issues affecting humankind, without taking recourse to the Scriptures or quoting earlier masters.

Notwithstanding his erudition and education, it is said that Krishnamurti had not read religious or philosophical treatises, imparting knowledge purely from first-hand insights and revelations.

Krishnamurti sought to "absolutely, unconditionally free" people from all forms of conditioning, asking everyone to simply *be* – this was the way to be in harmony with oneself, with others and with Nature. He stressed that the Truth could only be sought through personal realisation and not by blindly following any path, religion, sect or guru. The seeker had to strive himself to find the Truth, which was possible by discarding all forms of conditioning and stilling thoughts that hampered awareness of what *is*.

He didn't offer people any cut-and-dried solutions to their problems. Each person creates the environment that s/he lives in. All violence, suffering and human misery could end only if there was a transformation in the human psyche. Without this, all other means would prove futile.

This transformation would not come by seeking and following different gurus or paths. Each person had to look inward and understand his own mind in order to transcend its limitations.

Walking the Talk

Of Indian parentage, Krishnamurti never thought of himself as belonging to any particular country, community or religious sect. All such categorisations were illusory and divisive and the root cause of our problems. His teachings make it clear that man had to rise above religious dogmas and conditionings and adopt a meditative and spiritual approach to life. This was the only way to create a new civilisation where love, peace and compassion could be the guiding principles.

Man must realise he was a slave to his thoughts, which are always rooted in the past. Only when we become aware of this could one perceive the division between the thinker and the thought, the observer and the observed. It is then that we realise the illusory nature of this division and pure observation results. Insight through pure observation is timeless and independent of the past, he opined.

A seer in the truest sense of the term, he could foresee the problems that were to befall our planet decades before environment protection and sustainable development became major issues. In the 1970s itself, he voiced concern for human beings if computers were allowed to take over functions of the human brain.

He also recognised the importance of proper education for children, whereby they could learn to overcome societal conditionings. Toward this end, he opened schools in different countries, referring to these as places "where students and teachers can flower inwardly". Schools were not simply meant to "turn out human beings as mechanical, technological instruments – though jobs and careers are necessary – but also to flower as human beings, without fear, without confusion, with great integrity". For Krishnamurti, schools were meant to be "real centres of understanding, of comprehension, of life". Much before awareness about environmental issues was being put across to adults, he exhorted schoolchildren to treat the earth with care and sensitivity.

Krishnamurti didn't espouse any doctrine or philosophy. His writings, talks and discussions have, however, been compiled into 40 books, which are available in 47 languages.

With his peripatetic existence and regular public talks spread over six decades, Krishnamurti probably spoke to more people than any other human being in history. Although he spoke and wrote only in English, thousands of people would congregate to hear his public talks in Madras, Bombay, New Delhi, Ojai Valley (California), Saanen (Switzerland) and Brockwood Park (England).

On February 17, 1986 Jiddu Krishnamurti passed away at the age of 91. Seven Krishnamurti schools in India and the Krishnamurti Foundations now propagate the Master's thoughts and his core belief: *"Truth is a pathless land."*

For further information, contact:

Krishnamurti Foundation India

Vasanta Vihar

64 Greenways Road

Chennai – 600 028

INDIA

Tel: (044) 2493-7803/7596

E-mail: *publications@kfionline.org*

❑ ❑ ❑

OSHO RAJNEESH (1931–1990)

The Self-proclaimed 'God'

Here was one philosopher whom everybody either loved or hated. Which is exactly what Rajneesh wanted, as the last thing he liked was to be ignored. Two things stand out immediately about Rajneesh: he was India's most controversial guru and philosopher, as well as its most prolific, with around 600 published works.

Born at 5:13 in the evening on December 11, 1931 at Kuchwada in Madhya Pradesh, his real name was Chandra Mohan Jain. Although brought up as per Jain traditions during his childhood years, he never really subscribed to any particular faith all his life, charting his own course.

On March 21, 1953 he attained Enlightenment and later gave an elaborate account of this experience. He was just 21.

Having secured his Masters degree with first-class honours in philosophy from the University of Saugar in 1957, for nine years he taught philosophy at the University of Jabalpur, while simultaneously acting as a religious teacher. Old-time residents of Jabalpur recall Rajneesh cycling to the University sporting long locks even in those early years, establishing an aura of eccentricity amongst local residents.

Courting Controversy

In 1966, he chucked up his teaching job and shifted to Bombay, realising that teaching sannyasis was more like his calling. Acharya Rajneesh (as he was called initially) gave discourses to small groups of disciples at his apartment in Bombay. Even in those initial Bombay years, many of his disciples were foreigners.

Gradually, word of his controversial teachings began circulating. The effect was two-fold – on the one hand, it attracted hordes of the curious from India and abroad, while on the other hand, it raised the hackles of most conservative Bombayites and other Indians. By now, he had his sannyasis calling him 'Bhagwan' Rajneesh, which made his orthodox countrymen squirm in discomfort.

In 1974, Bombayites heaved a sigh of relief when Rajneesh moved to Pune, opening an ashram at the posh Koregaon Park. The move, Rajneesh claimed, was to ensure a larger ashram for his growing band of disciples, while critics felt it had more to do with the burgeoning opposition to his presence in Bombay.

The ashram at Koregaon Park was spread over six acres. By now, Rajneesh seemed to be gaining adherents by the minute, with his white followers seemingly outnumbering the Indians. Around this time, stories of "sexual orgies" began doing the rounds in Pune, which happens to be streets ahead in its conservative outlook compared to cosmopolitan Bombay. Murmurs of discontent were beginning to rise amongst Puneites, too. But Rajneesh and his saffron-clad disciples were seemingly oblivious to all this.

During his years on planet Earth, it is estimated that at least 50,000 foreigners may have visited his Koregaon Park ashram in their quest for spiritual enlightenment. Rajneesh preached an ecumenical spiritual path that absorbed elements of Hinduism, Zen Buddhism, Jainism, Christianity, Taoism, Sufism, and a host of other religious and philosophical tenets, including psychology, New Age therapies, Yoga and meditation. Many disciples were said to go into a trance and swoon at his mere touch. Trenchant critics whispered that the guru was putting hypnotic skills to good effect, a claim his disciples dismissed.

Express, Don't Repress

Rajneesh believed the way to salvation and Enlightenment was not through repressive means, but through expression and indulgence. Indeed, he proclaimed that man should indulge himself to his heart's content, until he was so sated that carnal pleasures no longer meant anything to him. This was the way to the state of "no past, no future, no attachment, no mind, no ego, no self".

He preached monism, saying God was everywhere, in everything and everyone. All people, good or bad, were intrinsically divine.

In 1979, he proclaimed that his movement was meant to preserve the human race: "If we cannot create the 'New Man' in the coming 20 years, then humanity has no future. The holocaust of a global suicide can only be avoided if a new kind of man can be created."

Resistance to Rajneesh now took a sinister turn. A knife-wielding man – said to be a "Hindu fundamentalist" – attacked the guru. The attacker was later identified as Vilas Tupe (today a small-time builder in Pune), who undertook the attack "because Rajneesh was a CIA agent"!

By this time, the income-tax authorities were also said to be making inquiries about the ashram. While all these events were unfolding, Rajneesh's health kept deteriorating, with the guru reportedly suffering from numerous ailments, including asthma and allergy.

Global Sojourn

Thanks to the stress of circumstances, Rajneesh and his large band of disciples left for the United States in 1981. It was hoped Rajneesh's health would improve abroad, with an array of better medical facilities available.

The group settled on a huge, 65,000-acre ranch near the town of Antelope, Oregon, which was purchased for $6 million. Naturally, the ranch was named Rajneeshpuram. Like they had done with the Koregaon Park land, the Rajneeshis transformed the barren valley into a lush, thriving town with a 4,500-foot paved airstrip, a 44-acre reservoir and all other amenities to support over 3,000 residents.

Here again, the local people were opposed to the presence of Rajneesh and his followers, dubbing them a "mind-control cult" run by a "sex guru". The townspeople ensured Rajneeshpuram was denied building permits; the sannyasis then went ahead with some constructions without approval. As their numbers increased, some sannyasis got themselves elected to the city council. Friction between the locals and the sannyasis kept rising by the day. Matters came to such a pass that soon there were murder charges against the sannyasis. Eventually some of them fled to Switzerland, where the group's bank accounts were.

There were also reports that the sannyasis had mixed salmonella in a local restaurant's food, to reduce a voter turnout that would have restricted the ashram's activities, and 751 people are supposed to have taken ill with food poisoning. Fearing that the law agencies would storm their premises (as would later happen at Waco, Texas, with another cult leader), his disciples had Rajneesh flown to safety to Charlotte, North Carolina.

Here, Rajneesh is said to have violated US immigration laws, when he arranged fake marriages between some Indian followers and American citizens so that the Indians obtained clearance to stay on in America. A charge of giving false information in his immigration papers was slapped on him.

As he spent time behind bars, his health deteriorated, and his concerned lawyers suggested he make an 'Alford Plea' (no-contest plea). This ensured a suspended sentence on condition that he left American shores.

In 1986, Rajneesh was back at the Pune ashram. His health continued to deteriorate and there were rumours that the American authorities may have poisoned him. It was now that Rajneesh changed his title for the last time, styling himself 'Osho', a Japanese term meaning 'master' or 'teacher'.

On January 19, 1990 Rajneesh succumbed to heart failure at his Pune commune.

Osho's Legacy

The most prolific seer in the history of mankind, Rajneesh has hundreds of books to his credit. Speaking of mankind's search for harmony, happiness and love, which lies at the core of all religious and spiritual thought, he gave discourses on Christianity, Buddhism, Sufism, Tao, Tantra, Sex, Yoga, the *Upanishads* and Zen, amongst a plethora of topics.

He also spoke on issues such as the meaning of life and death, the struggle for power and politics, the significance of science and education, understanding and harnessing the energy of sex and almost every other topic under the sun. Bound by no thought or tradition, he could passionately espouse a particular cause on one day, only to contradict that very topic and himself on some other day – with equal passion and vehemence!

Osho's discourses were later compiled into books and cassettes. Some of his books include: *The Book of Books, The Book of Wisdom, The Diamond Sutra, Dimensions Beyond the Known, The Divine Melody, The Path of Love, The Song of Ecstasy,*

Notes of a Madman, The Perfect Master, From Sex to Superconsciousness, Tantra, Spirituality & Sex, Absolute Tao, Finger Pointing to the Moon, Heartbeat of the Absolute, Vedanta: Seven Steps to Samadhi, The Way Beyond Any Way, Yoga: Science of the Soul, No-Mind: Flowers of Eternity, The Sun Rises in the Evening, and *Walking in Zen, Sitting in Zen.*

Strangely, once he had completed his "journey on earth", Rajneesh's countrymen began to take a more tolerant attitude towards him. During his heyday, his movement is said to have attracted over 200,000 adherents at 600 centres sprinkled across the globe. Even Rajneesh's own parents became his disciples. Unlike traditional gurus, Rajneesh lived a life of luxury and is purported to have had a collection of 93 Rolls Royces, supposedly gifted by disciples.

Although he refused to appoint any one person as his successor, a core group of 21 were assigned to look after the running of his ashram – now expanded to 32 acres – and other worldwide centres. Today, a stay at the ashram is only possible if one secures the mandatory AIDS negative certificate after being tested at the ashram.

A dozen years after his death, Osho's cassettes and books still attract thousands of adherents.

For further information, contact:

Osho Commune International

17 Koregaon Park

Pune – 411 001

INDIA

Tel: (20) 2401-9999

E-mail: *resort@osho.net*

❑❑❑

DIVINE PHILOSOPHY

SRI KRISHNA (3228–3102 BC)

The Divine Incarnation

Over 5,200 years ago, Lord Krishna was born at Vrindavan in the city of Mathura (about 80 miles from Delhi), in present-day Uttar Pradesh, on the banks of the Yamuna River. Sri Krishna was born to Devaki and Vasudeva in a prison cell of the tyrant Kansa. The reason for this unusual birthplace was a prediction by sage Narad that the eighth child of Devaki would slay Kansa. The story goes thus...

The Shooras were a branch of the brave Yadav clan, whose chief was Vasudeva. King Ugrasen ruled another clan that lived nearby. Ugrasen's first-born son was the evil Kansa. In order to maintain peace between the two tribes, elders from both tribes had forged a convenient marital alliance. Devak, King Ugrasen's brother, had a beautiful daughter, Devaki, who was married off to Vasudeva to ensure tribal peace.

On hearing of sage Narad's prediction, Kansa was consumed with rage. Not just the eighth child, he decided to kill every child of Devaki and Vasudeva immediately after they were born, to ensure there was no threat to his life whatsoever. The best way to go about this, he realised, was to have the couple put behind bars at his palace. Kansa thereby managed to kill six of Devaki's progeny. Vasudeva's kinsmen, however, smuggled out Devaki's seventh child immediately after His birth, to the nearby town of Gokul, where Vasudeva's friend, Nanda, lived. This child was Balarama.

When the eighth child was due, Devaki was filled with apprehension for its safety. However, it had already been predicted that Lord Vishnu would appear as her eighth child. On the appointed day, there was intense rain, thunder and lightning. Lord Vishnu then appeared in a vision before Vasudeva and informed him of His coming.

When Lord Krishna was born, the guards fell into a stupor and the prison gates opened of their own accord. Krishna was then taken across the Yamuna River to Gokul and left in the care of Nanda and his wife, Yashoda.

The Demon Slayer

As the child grew, He began his demon-killing spree. In fact, this was the purpose of His coming to earth. Legend has it that the gods and the demons had many battles in heaven. When the latter were defeated, they fled to earth, taking birth as princes in powerful royal families. Soon, these demons in human form began their quarrelsome activities on earth too, forcing the gods to invoke the help of Lord Vishnu.

Acceding to their request, Lord Vishnu descended to earth in the form of Sri Krishna. The Lord is said to have done this at various points of time, when evil had reigned supreme, in order to re-establish the teachings of the *Vedas*. *"Though I am the Unborn, the changeless Self..."* Sri Krishna reveals in the *Bhagavad Gita* (literally, *Song of God*), Chapter 4, Verse 7 and 8:

Yada yada hi dharmasya glanirbhavati Bharata,
Abhyutthanamadharmasya tadatmanam srijamyaham...

Whenever, O descendant of Bharat,
there is decline of Dharma,
and Adharma is in the ascendant,
then I body Myself forth.

For the protection of the virtuous,
for the destruction of evil-doers,
and for re-establishing dharma,
I am born from age to age.

Religious chroniclers say Sri Krishna was born on the midnight of the eighth day of the dark half of the Shravan month. As per the Gregorian calendar, this puts the birth date as July 19, 3228 BC. According to the accounts of the scholar Srila Vishvanatha Chakravarti, Sri Krishna spent the first three years and four months in Gokul. The same amount of time was spent in Vrindavan and Nandagram. For 18 years and four months He lived in Mathura. Finally, 96 years and eight months were spent in Dwarka, for a total of 125 years on earth.

Along with brother Balarama, His childhood years were spent under the care of His foster parents, Nanda and Yashoda, in the beautiful surroundings of Gokul, Vrindavan and Nandagram. When Krishna and Balarama were a little older, their evil uncle Kansa inveigled the brothers into a wrestling match with two big and powerful wrestlers who had been instructed to kill the duo. Krishna and Balarama, however, easily defeated the two wrestlers.

Subsequently, Krishna killed Kansa and Balarama slew his eight brothers. The pious King Ugrasen was then established as the emperor of several kingdoms.

Later, they spent time in Mathura, where they were taught the Gayatri Mantra by Garga Muni. Thereafter, they lived with Sandipani Muni, who taught them the Vedic arts and sciences in just 64 days and nights. The learning included military science, politics and spirituality.

It was when they were 90 years old that the great war of Kurukshetra took place, pitting the princes of Hastinapur against one another. Before the war, Sri Krishna gave both sides the option of either choosing Him as an advisor (without any active combat role) or of utilising the services of His army. While the wise Pandavas chose to have Sri Krishna on their side, the wily Kauravas opted to use the Lord's army.

Thereafter, Sri Krishna played the role of Arjuna's charioteer, exhorting the righteous Pandava prince into battle against his scheming cousins, the Kauravas.

Balarama, however, refused to participate in the hostilities in any way and went on a pilgrimage across India.

Doubts Vs Divine Wisdom

As both the formidable armies stood arrayed against each other, the brave Arjuna was inexplicably overcome by intense remorse, grief and fear. The sight of his own relatives, friends and teachers standing before him as enemies overwhelmed him with a deep sense of foreboding. Uneasy and deeply disturbed about the death and destruction that would inevitably follow the sounding of bugles, he laid down his arms and retreated to the back of the chariot.

On Sri Krishna's questioning, he revealed his intentions to retire to the forest rather than participate in the carnage of his near and dear ones. Arjuna said he was unable to lift his mighty bow, Gandiva, against his own blood. His love for his relatives clouded his sense of *dharma*, leaving him confused before the call of duty. In this moment of confusion, despair and helplessness, he turned to Sri Krishna, seeking His guidance. "How can I kill them? Will it not be proper to give up this whole kingdom, smacking of the blood of my own relatives, and retire to the forest in peace? O Krishna, I am unable to decide my plan of action. I surrender myself at Your holy feet. O Lord, please guide me through this difficult period."

Against this historic and dramatic background, the *Bhagavad Gita* then unfolded in the words of Sri Krishna. The Lord admonished Arjuna for his act of unmanliness and cowardice, telling him that for centuries to come people would remember this act and blame him for running away from the battlefield. For generations, he would be laughed at for his unmanly flight:

In such a crisis, whence comes upon thee,

O Arjuna, this dejection,

un-Aryan-like, disgraceful,

And contrary to the attainment of heaven?

Yield not to unmanliness, O son of Kunti!

Ill doth it become thee.

Cast off this mean faint-heartedness and arise,

O scorcher of thine enemies.

[Chapter 2, Verse 2 & 3]

This firm rebuke brought Arjuna around momentarily. His doubts continued to persist, though, and he still refused to fight against his own people.

Therefore, with the sword of wisdom

Cut off this doubt in your heart;

Follow the path of selfless action,

Stand up, Arjuna!

[Chapter 4, Verse 42]

Thereafter, their dialogue continued over long spells, with Arjuna placing his doubts and queries before Sri Krishna, who replied in words that have been immortalised for all time. The words of Sri Krishna that form the *Bhagavad Gita* are pearls of wisdom, the philosophy of philosophies that reveal the essence of the Unborn and the Imperishable.

I am the Self, Arjuna,

Seated in the heart of all beings;

I am the beginning and lifespan of beings,

and their end as well.

[Chapter 10, Verse 20]

In a total of 700 verses spanning 18 chapters, Sri Krishna dispelled Arjuna's doubts one at a time. The *Gita* is, in fact, considered to be a dialogue between man's lower Self and the Higher Self. The brave warrior asked and the Lord told him about man's goal in life, the purpose of human birth, about what the nature of one's duty or *dharma* should be, about the Self (Atman or soul) and about the three ways to attain salvation – *Jnana Yoga* (the way of knowledge), *Karma Yoga* (the way of action), and *Bhakti Yoga* (the way of devotion).

Thy right is to work only,

but never to the fruits thereof.

Be thou not the producer of the fruits of thy actions;

Neither let thy attachment be towards inaction.

[Chapter 2, Verse 47]

In this memorable dialogue, Sri Krishna tells Arjuna that he has to do his duty and fight the war without thinking about the consequences. Man has the right to do his duty, but no rights to the fruits thereof. As a Karma Yogi, a person should be committed to carrying out his allotted tasks without expectations of any fruits in return. Krishna reveals that work done selflessly, to the best of one's ability, is the best way for a worldly person to realise his Inner Self.

Only those persons may embrace a life of renunciation in whom recollections of past lives have created such a longing. Others in whom past impressions of sensual and sensory pleasures persist will still not be ready to accept the life of a sannyasi. Even if such people were to take to the path of sannyas, they would soon be ensnared in worldly activities and do more harm than good to the cause of spirituality. For people of such ilk, who happen to make up the majority, Sri Krishna advocates *Nishkam Karma Yoga* (the Yoga of selfless action) as the best path to realise the Truth. Selfless work done without expecting any benefits purifies the mind and leads to Ultimate Realisation and *moksha* or liberation.

Chapter 12 of the *Bhagavad Gita* speaks about the path of devotion – *Bhakti Yoga* – and lays stress on the qualifications and virtues of the *Bhakta* or follower.

In another verse, speaking about the real nature of man and the paths to seek the same, Sri Krishna reveals: *"O Arjuna, you are not this body, you are not this mind; you are ever pure, the unchanging eternal Self, Atman. This Atman is covered with the illusion of ignorance and comes to identify itself as a body-mind complex. Therefore, when you say 'you will kill them', or get killed by them, you are actually telling an untruth. The Atman is never killed, nor does it kill anybody."*

The Real Self

The body, Krishna explains, is just like clothes, which the Atman changes periodically, just as we change our old garments and wear new ones! Birth and death are inevitable. Just as death is assured for the born, birth is assured for the dead. Sri Krishna tells Arjuna that unlike him, who has forgotten all about his previous births, He can recall all His previous births.

By engaging in various spiritual activities, we can come to realise this Ultimate Truth. Control of the senses, renunciation, righteousness and a steady control of the mind help us realise the Ultimate Reality and become one with the Self or God.

Continues Sri Krishna:

Conquer thine enemies and

enjoy prospered kingship.

By Me Myself, they have already been slain long ago.

Be thou the mere instrument.

[Chapter 12, Verse 33]

Each time the Lord clears a particular doubt of Arjuna, his mind stumbles and wavers on another doubt. When Arjuna expresses his apprehension about being responsible for the death of his kinsmen, Sri Krishna reveals Himself in His *Virat Roop* – all-pervading Reality – beautifully described in Chapter 11. This Cosmic Form of Sri Krishna relates to three aspects: (1) *Shristi* or creation (2) *Sthiti* or maintenance (3) *Vinash* or destruction.

In His terrifying doomsday form, Arjuna sees the Lord swallowing the world. Warriors on both sides are already dead or dying. The awesome spectacle makes even the brave Arjuna shudder with fear. The Lord then reveals Himself in His most beautiful form and Arjuna is awash with a sense of bliss, beatitude, peace and serenity. Arjuna realises that death is but a temporary phenomenon like birth and, as part of the Immortal Self, he too is immortal.

In Chapter 18, the last one, Sri Krishna asks Arjuna, *"Are your doubts cleared, O Arjuna? Are you freed from the delusory ideas regarding your true nature?"*

Having just been blessed with Divine Knowledge, the grateful Arjuna replies: "Yes, my Lord. My ignorance has vanished. Destroyed is my delusion, and I have gained my memory through Thy Grace. O steadfast one, I am firm; my doubts are gone. Thy will be done."

After being blessed with Enlightenment through the Lord's grace, Arjuna's doubts finally vanished and he joined the battle.

The verses contained in the *Gita* are part of the highest knowledge available to mankind and an essence of the *Vedas* and the *Upanishads*. A part of the *Mahabharata*, the *Bhagavad Gita* ranks as one of the three most authoritative texts in Indian philosophical literature, along with the *Vedas* and the *Upanishads*.

Celestial Beacon

Having seen the inevitable outcome of the war, Arjuna thereafter did his duty. The Pandavas ultimately triumphed in this war. However, Gandhari – the mother of the slaughtered Kauravas – cursed Krishna for His role in the war, saying that His clan would die fighting amongst themselves.

Their missions having been completed, Krishna and Balarama returned to Dwarka. The next 35 years were spent in various activities, which are described in Sri Krishna's principal biography, *Srimad Bhagavatam* (*The Beautiful Book of God*).

Although the Lord manifests Himself in our material dimensions of time and space, He is the Unborn, the Unchanging and Immortal Spirit.

> *Foolish men conceive Me, the Unmanifest,*
> *as having become manifest.*
> *They do not know My higher nature,*
> *everlasting and supreme.*

[Chapter 7, Verse 24]

Almost 35 years later, as Gandhari had foretold, the Yadav clan in Dwarka fell to wanton ways and began fighting amongst themselves, exterminating one another.

Sri Krishna and Lord Balarama's mission on earth had by now been accomplished. Lord Balarama retired to the shore of the ocean. Legend has it that He then manifested a snake from His own mouth and rode off to the eternal abode.

Sri Krishna retired to the forest. As He lay resting in the jungle, a hunter shot an arrow tipped with poison, mistaking Him for a deer. The arrow struck Krishna in the leg and He left his mortal body on February 18, 3102 BC on the new moon night of *Phalgun*.

Sri Krishna's departure marks the beginning of *Kaliyug* or the age of corruption, which is said to be continuing to this day. The immortal words of Sri Krishna echoed in the *Bhagavad Gita*, however, still shine as brightly as they did over 5,000 years ago, serving as a beacon in these uncertain times.

❑ ❑ ❑

Books on ________ Great People and Inspirational Quotes

Postage Extra